THE AMERICAN SERIES
of
FOREIGN PENAL CODES

5

THE TURKISH CODE OF CRIMINAL PROCEDURE

The
TURKISH CODE
OF
CRIMINAL PROCEDURE

With an Introduction by

Dr. Feyyaz Gölzüklü

Docent of Criminal Law Procedure
Political Science Faculty
Ankara University

Introduction translated by

Professor Yilmaz Altuğ

Docent of Private International Law
Faculty of Law
Istanbul University

FRED B. ROTHMAN & CO.
SOUTH HACKENSACK, N.J.

SWEET & MAXWELL LIMITED
LONDON

Translated by

LEGAL RESEARCH INSTITUTE
Faculty of Law
Ankara University

NEW YORK UNIVERSITY FACULTY TEAM
Ankara University

JUDGE ADVOCATE'S OFFICE,
JOINT UNITED STATES MILITARY MISSION FOR
AID TO TURKEY

WILLIAM BELSER
with the co-operation of
PROFESSOR YILMAZ ALTUĞ
Istanbul University
and
PROFESSOR TUGRUL ANSAY
Ankara University

Editorial Assistance

PROFESSOR CHARLES TENNEY
Boston University

MUSTAFA T. YÜCEL
New York University

Editor-in-Chief

GERHARD O. W. MUELLER

THE AMERICAN SERIES OF FOREIGN PENAL CODES

1. THE FRENCH PENAL CODE
2. THE KOREAN CRIMINAL CODE
3. THE NORWEGIAN PENAL CODE
4. THE GERMAN PENAL CODE
5. THE TURKISH CODE OF CRIMINAL PROCEDURE

*PUBLICATIONS OF THE COMPARATIVE CRIMINAL LAW
PROJECT*

1. ESSAYS IN CRIMINAL SCIENCE

Published in the U.S.A.
by Fred B. Rothman & Co.
of 57 Leuning Street,
South Hackensack,
New Jersey

Published in Great Britain
by Sweet & Maxwell Limited
of 11 New Fetter Lane,
London, Law Publishers

Printed in Great Britain
by
The Eastern Press Ltd. of London and Reading

CONTENTS

CODE OF CRIMINAL PROCEDURE
(April 4, 1929)
Statute #1412

BOOK I
GENERAL PROVISIONS

BOOK II
PROCEDURAL REQUIREMENTS

Contents

PREFACE

IF there ever was a project for the accomplishment of which a great many people deserve equal credit, this translation of the Turkish Code of Criminal Procedure has that distinction. In the Fall of 1956 it had become obvious to the Judge Advocate General's Office, JUSMMAT, Ankara, Turkey, and to the Legal Research Institute of the University of Ankara, that some basic translations of Turkish laws into English should be made in the field of criminal jurisprudence. Through the co-operation of Colonel Charles Lawrence and Captain Wade Williamson of JUSMMAT, and Professors Delmar Karlen, Kenneth Redden and Frederick Davis, of New York University, School of Law, then on duty with the Legal Research Institute, a co-operative of several competent translators was formed, and a translation of the Turkish Code of Criminal Procedure resulted in 1957. These translators are Professor Ilhan Lütem of the Ankara University Law Faculty, Miss Nerriman Seymen, and Miss Uren Arsan of the staff of the Legal Research Institute, and Mr. Orhan Sepiçi and Mr. Mustafa Ovaçik, members of the Legal Section of the JUSMMAT Translation Branch. Mr. Sepiçi and Mr. Ovaçik also checked the entire manuscript for accuracy and errors in substance.

This translation was published in mimeographed form, jointly by the Legal Research Institute, Faculty of Law, Ankara University, and the New York University Graduate School of Public Administration and Social Science, in co-operation with the Judge Advocate's Office, JUSMMAT. Through the good offices of Professor Joseph W. Hawley of New York University, then co-director of the Legal Research Institute of the Faculty of Law, Ankara University, the Comparative Criminal Law Project of New York University obtained the permission of the Legal Research Institute and of the office of the Judge Advocate, through Col. Walter J. Rankin, to perfect the translation and to publish it in the Project's American Series of Foreign Penal Codes. This last phase of the work was accomplished with the kind help of Professor Tugrul Ansay, Ankara University and University of the

ix

Middle East, Professor Nevzat Gürelli and Professor Yilmaz Altuğ, University of Istanbul, Mr. Mustafa T. Yücel, an alumnus of both Ankara University and New York University Schools of Law, and Professor Charles W. Tenney, Jr. (LL.M., N.Y.U. 1961). The introduction to this volume was written by Dr. Feyyaz Gölzüklü of Ankara University, and translated by Professor Yilmaz Altuğ. To all of them the Comparative Criminal Law Project owes a debt of deep gratitude for a job well done. As customary, the editor-in-chief has exercised the right to select final terminology and, thus, it is he who assumes the responsibility for all conceivable inaccuracies. The usual policies governing the translations of the Project have also been applied to this work.

This publication is significant for a variety of reasons. It is a splendid example of international co-operation among colleagues in private and government agencies. It is the first English translation of any foreign code of criminal procedure, permitting the English-speaking criminal lawyer his first direct glance at a civilian code of criminal procedure. It is the translation of a work with a sociologically most interesting background. Originally alien to the Turkish people—resting largely on the German Code of Criminal Procedure of 1877—this code was splendidly adapted to and adopted by the Turkish people. It is, lastly, a work of translation which should be of direct practical benefit to those Turks and Americans who in civil friendship and military alliance are working for a common goal.

GERHARD O. W. MUELLER.

New York University,
1961.

INTRODUCTION

THE Turkish Code of Criminal Procedure of April 20, 1929 (Law No. 1412), as it is still in force today, and which is reproduced in its entirety on the following pages, is a translation of the German Code of Criminal Procedure of 1877, adopted with some changes. The Turkish Code was amended by the Laws of June 16, 1936; June 7, 1937; June 28, 1938 and January 30, 1942. A separate Law, of June 8, 1936, provided a special procedure for "flagrant offenses." The flagrant offenses, punishable by heavy penalty, had been left out of the original version. Under the Law of June 27, 1938, within the scope of the above-mentioned statute of June 8, 1936, they are now includable under certain circumstances.

The Turkish Code of Criminal Procedure adopted the so-called mixed system of Criminal Procedure. As will be seen, the preparation of public prosecution and preliminary investigation are conducted secretly, in the suspect's absence, and as a matter of record (Art. 180 *et seq.*), in accordance with the inquisitorial system. The remaining procedure is conducted publicly, in the accused's presence and orally, according to the accusatorial system (Arts. 373, 374, 240, 238, 242).

Turkish procedural law contains many provisions for securing the independence and impartiality of the judges and the courts. Moreover, the independence from the executive branch of government is secured by the adoption of the principle of separation of powers (Constitution, Arts. 8, 54, 57), and through prohibition of dismissal of judges. The appointment, promotion and punishment of judges are governed by provisions separate from those governing other civil servants (Law of Judges, of June 4, 1943, Law No. 2556). To secure this independence, the institutions of the jury and the lay assessor court, which can be found in some foreign countries, were not accepted into the Turkish judicial organization. The independence within the judiciary is secured through the absence of a hierarchic relation between judges and courts and the acceptance of the principles of separation of the offices of prosecution, investigation and trial.

The immunity of judges against parties litigant for their decisions is adopted as a general principle, thus securing their

1

independence before the parties. While there are exceptions to the general rule, they are very few and narrowly defined (Arts. 573–576, Code of Civil Procedure).

The disqualification of a possibly biased judge (*e.g.*, for kinship) and his disqualification on his own motion or on the motion of the parties, are examples of such measures to secure his impartiality.

Turkish judicial organization accepts the principle of the unity of civil and criminal justice, *i.e.*, civil and criminal cases are tried by the same judges and courts. Furthermore, there are no intermediate courts of appeals, or of second instance. Only the Court of Appeals reviews the appeals from all trial courts.

Turkish criminal courts are of two types, general and special courts. Justice of the Peace Courts, Courts of General Criminal Jurisdiction (Asliye) and Aggravated Felony Courts are the general courts (Introductory Statute to the Code of Criminal Procedure, Art. 25 *et seq.*). The Justice of the Peace Courts try persons charged with misdemeanors strictly as listed in the Criminal Code (Introductory Statute to the Code of Criminal Procedure, Art. 29). The Aggravated Felony Courts try persons charged with felonies punishable by severe punishment (death, severe imprisonment and imprisonment for more than five years, Art. 421). All offenses outside these two groups are subject to the jurisdiction of the Criminal Courts of General Jurisdiction. Justice of the Peace Courts and Courts of General Criminal Jurisdiction have one judge. Aggravated Felony Courts have a Chief Justice and two Associate Justices. Above these three types of courts there is the Court of Appeals (Temyiz Mahkemesi). The five criminal departments of this Court have their jurisdiction defined according to the subject-matter of the review. Generally speaking, the Justice of the Peace Courts and the Criminal Courts of General Jurisdiction are located in the district (Kaza) capitals and the Aggravated Felony Courts are located in the provincial (vilayet) capitals. The Supreme Court (of Appeals), which secures the unity of jurisdiction and the uniformity in legal interpretation throughout the country, located in Ankara, reviews only questions of law and its proper application.

The Supreme Divan (Yüce Divan), composed of twenty-one judges selected from among the members of the Supreme Court (of Appeals) and the Council of State, has jurisdiction over the trial of Ministers, the presidents and members of the Council of State, and of the Supreme Court (of Appeals) as well as the Chief Public Prosecutor (the Public Prosecutor of the Supreme Court (of Appeals)) for offenses committed in the performance of their duties. Military Courts try military personnel and military offenses. Both the Supreme Divan and the Military Courts are special courts outside the general judiciary.

Juvenile courts have not yet been established in our country.

The jurisdiction and venue of courts are limited by subject-matter (*ratione materiae*), locality (*ratione loci*), and person (*ratione personae*), thus limiting as well as protecting the judge. Therefore, courts cannot try any cases outside their jurisdiction. However, there are exceptions, such as the disposal by a court of higher jurisdiction, under certain circumstances, of a case over which a court of lower jurisdiction has original jurisdiction (Arts. 2, 3, 4 and 262); the joinder of cases for connected offenses in any court with power to try any of them (Art. 12); the transfer of a case to another court of equal rank when for legal or factual reasons a judge or a court having jurisdiction is unable to perform his or its judicial duties, or if the investigation cannot be conducted without prejudice to the public safety at the place where the action is pending.

The court which has venue is the court of the place where the offense has been committed. If this place is unknown, the court of the place where the accused is seized has venue. If he is not seized, the court of his place of domicile, and if he is not domiciled in Turkey, the court of the place where he last resided in Turkey, has venue. If, despite the foregoing rules, it is still impossible to determine the proper court, then the court which took the initiative in the criminal proceeding shall have venue (Arts. 8, 9). The court having venue over offenses committed in foreign countries, but which should be prosecuted in Turkey according to Articles 4, 5, 6, 7, 8 of the Criminal Code, is determined according to the above-mentioned rules (Art. 10). If an offense is committed on a vessel or aircraft bearing the Turkish flag on the high seas, or in the air, or in a foreign port, or foreign territorial waters, or if the crime is committed by means of such a vessel or aircraft, the court of the port of first arrival of the vessel or aircraft in Turkey, after the commission of the offense, or the court of the place of registry of the vessel or aircraft, shall have venue (Art. 11).

Jurisdictional rules are rules of public policy and their application is obligatory; the parties cannot stipulate against them. A possible conflict of jurisdiction between several courts is resolved, in general, by the common court of higher jurisdiction (Arts. 13, 18, and Introductory Statute to the Code of Criminal Procedure, Art. 36).

All offenses are prosecuted in the name of the People, by public prosecutors who are virtually representatives of the executive branch of Government within the judiciary (Arts. 147, 148). There is a public prosecutor with deputies of a number determined by necessity at every Court of General Criminal Jurisdiction. The function of the public prosecutor of the Aggravated Felony Court is performed by the public prosecutor of the Court of General Criminal Jurisdiction of that locale. There is no public prosecutor at the Justice of the Peace Courts. However, proceedings in these courts likewise are initiated by accusation of the public prosecutor of the Criminal Court of General Jurisdiction. He is not present at the trial, but communicates his opinion in writing. Nevertheless, in some lighter offenses, as specifically defined by law, and where there is more injury to private persons than to the public, the persons injured by the offense may institute direct criminal proceedings by filing a private complaint without participation by the public prosecutor's office (Art. 344). In this exceptional case the civil complainant, who has the qualification of a real party in interest, enjoys all rights recognized by law. Furthermore, the person injured by the offense may intervene in any public prosecution initiated by the public prosecutor, and may there claim from the criminal court an adjudication of his personal claims, in addition to the punishment. He is a party to the action in the nature of an intervenor (Art. 365).

An arrest, temporarily limiting the freedom of the defendant, who, after all, is merely the " opposing party " in the criminal suit, may be had only by judicial decisions and in accordance with the forms and under the conditions prescribed by law. During the preparation of public prosecution the warrant of arrest is issued by a Justice of the Peace, during the preliminary examination by the investigating magistrate in charge of the investigation, and during the trial by the trial court (Arts. 124, 125, 158). Arrests are, on principle, without time limit, but the arrestee can object to the warrant of arrest at every stage and instance of the investigation (Arts. 111, 112), and the warrant of arrest is subject to periodic examinations. At periodic intervals the investigating magistrate examines *ex officio* the expediency of continued detention in the house of detention. Such an examination must be made within thirty days from the date of the arrest of the accused. If the investigating magistrate, upon examination, decides not to release the accused, he will at that time set another date for further review of the necessity of detention. Subsequent examinations are made at intervals of not less than three weeks nor more than two months, but, upon the accused's request for an examination, they may be held at more frequent intervals. Examinations and reviews of the same nature, but during trial, are conducted within the same intervals (Art. 112). The warrant of arrest may be withdrawn at any time when the grounds for an arrest no longer subsist (Art. 123), and release on bail is possible at every stage of the investigation. As a matter of fact, there is no obligatory arrest and the public prosecutor does not have any authority to arrest the accused. The arrest of an accused may be ordered only when there are strong indications of guilt, and facts indicating that the accused is attempting to remove evidence or that there is danger that the accused might escape, or when the offense is one against the authority of the state or the government or against the security of the public or against public morals (Art. 104). When the offense of which the accused is suspected is a felony, or when the accused has no domicile or residence, or is a vagrant, a suspicious character or unable to identify himself, or when the accused is a foreigner and there are strong indications that he would neither respond to a summons nor surrender for the execution of the judgment, the accused is irrebuttably presumed to plan an escape. An arrest for misdemeanor is exceptional and limited by very tight restrictions (Art. 105).

An arrested person is immediately arraigned before the judge who ordered the arrest and judicially examined not later than on the day following the arrest (Art. 108).

In cases where a delay would be detrimental, and under the circumstances prescribed by the law, the accused may be temporarily arrested without the warrant of arrest. When the offender is discovered in the commission of the offense (*flagrante delicto*) or in immediate pursuit, and if there is reason to fear that he will attempt to escape, or if it is impossible otherwise to identify such a person, he may be temporarily placed under arrest by anyone without a warrant. Public prosecutors and police officers who lack the opportunity to report to their superiors, may temporarily arrest an accused in cases where the issuance of a warrant of arrest is imminent and a delay would be detrimental. "Flagrant offenses" are those interrupted during their commission, those whose commission has just been observed, those committed by persons while under pursuit by the police, the victim, or others, those evidenced immediately before the apprehension of the perpetrator by the existence of stolen goods or other evidence of the commission of a crime, and those where such goods as evidence are found on or with the person of the perpetrator (Art. 127). The arrested person is taken before the judge without delay and is examined no later than the day following his arrest (Art. 128).

In a criminal prosecution the defendant has the right to seek the advice and assistance of a defense counsel (Arts. 138 and 141). Since the preparation of public prosecutions and preliminary investigation are being conducted in privacy (secretly), the defense counsel cannot examine the investigation files and cannot accompany the accused in the preliminary examination (Art. 185).

The burden of proving the guilt of the defendant rests on the public prosecutor or the private claimant; in other words, the defendant is considered not guilty until guilt is established by final judgment.

In the law of evidence the system of the "intimate conviction" of the trier of fact has been adopted. The judge considers the probative value of all evidence submitted to him from the investigatory phase and during trial, freely attributing credence, to the best of his conscience (Art. 254). But, for the proof of guilt, definite evidence must be used, *i.e.*, confession, testimony of witnesses, writings and records of officials, evidence gained through discovery, judicial notice, searches and seizures, and the opinions of experts, from all of which the judge may obtain information on the offense and the offender. Each of these means of proof mentioned are stipulated in detail by law in order to prevent abuses and to strengthen the belief in the manifestation of truth.

The public prosecutor, who is informed of the occurrence of a crime, makes a preliminary investigation in order to decide whether it is necessary to institute a public prosecution and to ascertain the identity of the person who committed it. During this investigation the judicial (state's attorney's) police aid him. As long as the perpetrator of a crime remains unknown, no criminal prosecution can be opened. If at the end of the preparation for public prosecution the public prosecutor reaches the conclusion that a public prosecution is necessary, he institutes a case either by making an accusation or by giving a written demand to the examining judge for the opening of a preliminary investigation (Arts. 163, 192). Otherwise, the public prosecutor renders a decision not to prosecute and informs the civil complainant, if any, who filed charges (Art. 164). The Minister of Justice, by order, also may direct the public prosecutor to initiate a public prosecution. However, a public prosecutor who has to initiate a public prosecution upon order of the Minister of Justice, is subsequently free in his decisions (Art. 148). Interested parties have the right to object to the prosecutor's decision not to prosecute (Art. 165), and if such petitioner is also a victim, he may do so within fifteen days after notice to the president of the nearest Aggravated Felony Court, and direct his objection to the Aggravated Felony Court with which the public prosecutor is connected. The objection must be accompanied by facts and proofs which justify the opening of prosecution and must be signed by an attorney. If there are insufficient grounds to justify the commencement of a public prosecution, the chief justice refuses the petition and informs the parties accordingly. After such an action, a public prosecution may be opened only for newly discovered facts and evidence (Art. 167). If the chief justice is convinced that the petition is valid and supported, he orders the opening of the public prosecution. The public prosecutor must comply with this decision (Art. 168).

The preliminary investigation is conducted by the investigating magistrate to determine whether there is a necessity for trial (Art. 177). According to the Turkish Code of Criminal Procedure, preliminary investigation is obligatory in matters of aggravated felonies, and is discretionary in matters within the jurisdiction of Courts of General Criminal Jurisdiction. There is no preliminary investigation as to matters within the jurisdiction of the Justice of the Peace Courts.

If at the end of the preliminary investigation a decision for the commencement of trial is rendered, this decision is sent with the accusation of the public prosecutor to the court of venue. Otherwise, upon the decision to dismiss the charges, the file is closed and the investigation terminated.

Other possible decisions to be rendered at the end of the preliminary investigation are the temporary suspension of the trial (disappearance of the accused, or his unfitness to proceed for reasons of mental illness, incurred after commission of the crime), or lack of permission to prosecute where prosecution is subject to permission; a decision to the effect that venue or jurisdiction of the court over the subject-matter or over the person are lacking; the postponement of the trial and the decision to drop the case.

Final investigation (trial) commences on the date previously set for trial, at a designated court room and after the formation of the court in accordance with law and in the presence of the parties. Evidence is submitted to the court in the manner prescribed by statute and then contested. The trial cannot proceed if the defendant does not appear in court (Art. 223). Administrative matters and the preservation of order in the court are the concern of the chief justice (Art. 231). The trial commences with a roll-call of the witnesses and experts. Thereafter, the identity of the accused is registered. This is followed by a reading of the decision on the opening of trial in all cases in which a preliminary investigation had taken place, and a reading of the accusation in cases where there had been no preliminary investigation, followed by the questioning of the defendant (Art. 236). This is followed by the introduction of evidence (Art. 237). After the defendant has heard the witnesses, experts or accomplices, and after the reading of any document, he is asked whether he wants to challenge any such evidence (Art. 250). Upon completion of the introduction and adjudication of evidence, the civil complainant has the right to speak, after him the public prosecutor, thereafter the person with a property interest and finally the accused. The public prosecutor has the right to answer the defendant, and the defendant and his counsel have the right to reply to the public prosecutor. The defendant has to make the last statement. Even if he has been defended by counsel, he is asked to make a last statement personally, if he so desires (Art. 251). The trial ends with the rendition of the judgment, consisting of two parts, the judgment proper, or decision, and the justification of the judgment (Art. 260 *et seq.*).

Final investigation (trial) is open to the public (Art. 373). However, the court may decide, for reasons of protecting public morals and security, to hold a partly or completely closed session (Arts. 373, 374, 375). The trials of children under fifteen years of age must be conducted in closed sessions (Art. 375). Publication of trials conducted in closed sessions is forbidden (Art. 377).

All phases of final investigation (trial) are conducted in the presence of the defendant, including all formalities of procedure and especially the proof of guilt (Art. 240). The Turkish Code of Criminal Procedure has adopted the method of trial *in absentia* as an exception only in cases where light sentences are involved; *i.e.*, where the offense is punishable by fine, light imprisonment, confiscation or any combination thereof, the trial may proceed even if the defendant does not appear in court. On his own motion, a defendant may be excused from attending trial, except where the crime carries a serious punishment. If such motion is granted, and if the defendant has not been questioned during the preliminary investigation, he will be questioned as to the principal facts of the case by *letters rogatory* (Arts. 225, 226). The defendant may send a defense counsel in cases where his presence is not necessary (Art. 227). Trial may also be instituted against an absentee defendant who resides in a foreign country or whose place of residence is unknown, when it is evident that he cannot be brought before the court or that the service of summons would be useless, and when the offense involves fine or confiscation or both (Arts. 269, 270).

Final investigation (trial) is oral. During the trial all procedural transactions are concluded orally; the accused, witnesses and experts are examined by the court. Records are read aloud. The court must have direct access to all evidence (Arts. 238, 242, 244, 249).

The trial is held without interruption in the presence of the judges who will take part in formulating the judgment (Art. 219). In cases of necessity, however, the trial may be adjourned or suspended (Arts. 221, 222).

During both the preliminary investigation and the trial, the investigating magistrate and the court have authority to introduce evidence; they need not satisfy themselves solely with the evidence introduced by the parties.

All judgments denying any motion and all decisions against which there lies a remedy of law must contain a reasoned justification or explanation.

Remedies of law are of two kinds: those which prevent the finality of a decision or judgment; and those which may lead to the amendment of a final judgment. Exception (Art. 297 *et seq.*) and appeal (Art. 305 *et seq.*) belong to the first group, while reversal by a written order (Art. 343), new trial in favor of accused (Art. 327), correction of the decision and the chief public prosecutor's protest to a decision given by one of the criminal departments of the court, belong to the second group.

Except as otherwise prescribed by law, exceptions may be taken against the decisions of the investigating magistrate, those empowered to take depositions, and those of a chief or associate justice of the Court of General Criminal Jurisdiction, and of the Justice of the Peace Court, but not if the decision is part of the regular trial proceedings. No exceptions can be taken against the final decisions of the court (Arts. 297, 298). Authority to review exceptions is given by Article 299 of the Code.

The judgments of criminal courts may be appealed. Sentences restricting liberty for fifteen years or more, as well as death sentences, are reviewed by the Supreme Court (of Appeals), on its own motion and without any charges or expenses (Art. 305). Decisions rendered before judgment and forming the basis for the judgment may be appealed together with the judgment (Art. 306). An appeal may be made only for the reason that the judgment is contrary to law. Non-application or wrong application of a legal rule is a violation of law (Art. 307). Upon request, convictions of offenses punishable by serious punishments are reviewed before the Supreme Court (of Appeals) in the presence of the parties (Art. 318).

A judgment reversed by the Supreme Court (of Appeals) is sent either to the originating court or to another court of the same degree of jurisdiction for a new trial (Arts. 321, 322).

In the situations prescribed by Article 322, the Supreme Court (of Appeals) renders its decision on the merits of the case.

When the Minister of Justice is informed of violations of law in the decisions and judgments rendered by judges and courts, which become final without review by the Supreme Court (of Appeals), he orders the Chief Public Prosecutor's Office, in writing, to apply to the Supreme Court (of Appeals) for the reversal of the decision or judgment (Art. 343).

Under the circumstances prescribed in Article 322, a case which has been concluded by final judgment may be reheard by way of a new trial, and such a new trial may also be had against the defendant (Art. 330).

The Chief Public Prosecutor may protest the decision of any one of the Criminal Departments of the Supreme Court (of Appeals), at the General Criminal Board of the Supreme Court (of Appeals), within thirty days after the court decree has been submitted.

A procedural remedy against the decision of the Criminal Departments or the General Criminal Board is available only during appellate review, when points specified in an appellate petition, brief or notification have been omitted, and/or errors which will directly affect the essence of the judgment. The authority to request a corrective decision lies with the Chief Public Prosecutor (Art. 322).

A Justice of the Peace may impose punishment by issuing a penal decree without a hearing on matters which rest within his (misdemeanor) jurisdiction. Punishments thus imposed are only light fines, light imprisonment not exceeding three months, and suspension of a certain profession or trade, if necessary (Art. 386). If the person thus convicted objects to the decree, it is then vacated and the defendant is tried in the normal way, with a hearing (Arts. 390, 391).

Flagrant offenses, as above defined, may be tried by a summary procedure of trial, under special law (Statute No. 3006, of June 8, 1936, and June 27, 1938). The law on the trial of flagrant offenses fixes the forms and conditions of the application of this procedure.

Dr. Feyyaz Gölzüklü
*Docent of Criminal
Law and Procedure,
Political Science Faculty,
Ankara University, 1961.*

Translated by:
Professor Yilmaz Altug
*Docent of Private
International Law,
Faculty of Law,
Istanbul University, 1961.*

CODE OF CRIMINAL PROCEDURE

Official Gazette   (April 4, 1929)   Statute   #1412
1172—4/20/29.

BOOK I

GENERAL PROVISIONS

CHAPTER 1

JURISDICTION

1. Jurisdiction

The jurisdiction of the courts shall be determined by law.

2. Joinder and Separation of Actions

Connected criminal cases, even where, if separately considered, they ordinarily would be triable in different courts, may be disposed of in a single proceeding by the court of higher jurisdiction.

Nevertheless, such court may decide on the separation of cases which were joined.

3. Connected Offenses

Cases are deemed to be connected for the purposes of the preceding section if the accused is charged with more than one crime or if two or more persons are charged with having committed the same crime.

4. Joinder and Separation of Cases During the Investigation

Even after the commencement of the investigation, joinder or severance may be ordered by the court either on its own motion or on that of the accused or the public prosecutor. The competent court for such an order is the highest court having jurisdiction.

5. Procedure Applicable to Joined Cases

In joined cases, the procedure to be applied will be that appropriate to the highest court where the action is being tried.

6. Offenses Committed by Military Personnel

Offenses committed by military personnel, not involving a military duty and which are not otherwise military offenses and which are not committed against military personnel, are tried by the ordinary courts.

15

Whenever civilians are involved in offenses committed by military personnel not involving a military duty, the trial of such offenses shall take place in the ordinary courts.

Trial of non-military personnel always takes place in the ordinary courts.

7. Decision on Jurisdiction on the Court's Own Motion

A court may decide, at any stage of the proceedings, on its own motion, whether it has jurisdiction over the case or not.

CHAPTER 2

VENUE

8. Venue

The trial of a criminal action shall be held in the place where the offense was committed.

In cases of criminal attempts, or continuing or successive offenses, the place where the last act was committed shall be the place of the trial.

In the event of an offense committed by means of publication within Turkey, the place of publication shall be the place of the trial.

Nevertheless, where a private complaint is a requirement to the prosecution for defamation or insult, the place of trial may be set in the place where the complainant resides provided that the publication was distributed in that place.

9. Special Cases: Venue

If the place where the offense was committed is unknown, the court of the place where the accused is seized, or, if he is not seized, the court of his place of domicile shall have venue.

If the accused does not reside in Turkey, the court of the place where he last resided in Turkey has venue.

If, despite the foregoing rules, it is still impossible to determine which is the proper court, then the court exercising the first procedural step in the criminal proceeding shall have venue.

10. Venue over Extra-Territorial Offenses

Venue over offenses committed outside of Turkey but which should be prosecuted in Turkey according to Articles 4, 5, 6, 7 and 8 of the Criminal Code, is determined according to the first and second paragraphs of the preceding article.

However, upon the request of either the Public Prosecutor or the accused, the Court of Cassation may fix venue in the court nearest to the place where the offense was committed.

If in such cases the accused is not seized in Turkey or has no known residence or domicile in Turkey, venue is determined by the Court of Cassation upon request of the Minister of Justice and petition of the Chief Public Prosecutor.

The only courts which have venue over personal offenses of Turkish Government Officials residing in foreign countries and benefiting therein from diplomatic immunity are those of Ankara.

11. Offenses Committed on or by Means of Maritime Vessels and Aircraft

If an offense is committed on a maritime vessel or aircraft bearing the Turkish flag on the high seas, or in the air, or in a foreign port or foreign territorial waters, or, if the crime is committed by means of such a vessel or aircraft, the court where the action is brought is the court of the port of first arrival in Turkey after the commission of the offense, or the court of the place where it is registered.

12. Venue with Respect to Connected Offenses

Connected criminal cases, each of which would normally be tried before courts in different places according to the preceding articles, may be joined and tried in any court that has power to try either one of them.

If each one of the connected criminal cases is already in the process of being tried in different courts, all or some of them may be joined before one of the courts upon an agreement reached among those courts provided that it is in accordance with the request of the Public Prosecutor.

If an agreement is not reached, then upon request of the Public Prosecutor or the accused, a court of higher jurisdiction may decide whether it is necessary to join the cases and, if so, before which court.

Severance of actions is effected in the same way.

13. Affirmative Conflict of Venue

If a conflict arises between several judges or courts, each claiming the right to try a given case, the common court of higher jurisdiction shall determine which judge and court has to exercise the right of venue.

14. Transfer of a Case

If for legal or factual reasons a judge or a court having venue is unable to perform its judicial duties, or if the performance of investigation in the place where the action is pending is prejudicial to the public security, the court of higher jurisdiction may transfer the action to another court of the same degree in a different location.

Transfer of the case for reasons of public security is requested by the Minister of Justice.

15. Challenging the Venue

The accused must challenge the venue before the completion of the preliminary investigation. However, if no preliminary investigation has been performed, the accused must object at the commencement of the trial and before the public prosecutor's accusation is read.

16. Scope of Venue Rulings During Preliminary Investigation

A ruling on venue made during the preliminary investigation is binding as to venue insofar as subsequent proceedings are concerned.

17. Decision on Rejection of Venue

A decision upon the request of the accused as to the rejection of venue shall be made before the reading of the court's decision on the commencement of trial, or, before the reading of the accusation. Thereafter the Public Prosecutor cannot challenge the court's venue nor can the court inquire into venue on its own motion.

18. Rejection of Venue: Conflicts

Where two or more courts or investigating judges decline to act for reasons of lack of venue when one of them should have venue and it is otherwise impossible to appeal against such rulings, the common court of higher jurisdiction shall determine which court or investigating judge shall have venue.

19. Effect of Lack of Venue

Investigation proceedings of a court or investigating judge

undertaken without proper venue are not void merely because such venue was lacking.

20. Where Consideration of Venue Questions Would Result in Prejudicial Delay

A court or an investigating judge shall perform investigation within its judicial locality, even where venue is lacking, when delay in proceedings would be prejudicial to a just disposition of the case.

CHAPTER 3

DISQUALIFICATION OF A JUDGE

21. Circumstances of Disqualification

In the following instances a judge is not qualified to discharge his duties:

(1) If the judge himself has been affected by the crime.

(2) If the relation of marriage or guardianship exists or previously existed between the judge and the accused.

(3) If between the judge and either the accused or the injured party there exists kinship in the direct line (descendants and ascendants) including adopted persons, or if between the judge and either the accused or an injured party there exists a direct relationship including the third degree relationships, or kinship to the second degree even in the collateral line, including relationships resulting from dissolved marriages.

(4) If in the same suit the judge has acted as Public Prosecutor, criminal officer, or counsel for the accused or counsel for an injured party.

(5) If in the same suit the judge has acted as a witness or an expert witness.

22. Judges Prohibited from Joining in the Judgment

A judge who participated in the decision against which an appeal is made cannot participate in the decision given by the Superior Court.

Neither the investigating judge nor any judge who previously gave any decision in the case can participate in the final investigation.

23. Conditions Permitting a Party to Move for Disqualification and Those Entitled to so Move

Disqualification of a judge may be requested in those instances where he is not qualified to discharge his judicial functions and also where there exist circumstances which raise doubts concerning his impartiality.

The Public Prosecutor, the accused, or the plaintiff are entitled to move for disqualification.

The names of the judges who will participate in the judgment will be furnished to anyone of the aforesaid parties when requested.

24. Timeliness of Motion to Disqualify Judge on Grounds Which Raise Doubts Concerning his Impartiality

A motion for disqualification on grounds of suspected partiality of a judge may be made at any time before the final decision to open trial or the accusation is read, and in the event of an appeal the motion to disqualify an appellate judge may be made at any time before the presentation of the rapporteur's report in those cases where there is a hearing, and in cases where there is no hearing, the motion can be made at any time before the initiation of the appellate review.

Where the circumstances entitling one to move for disqualification arise subsequent to the aforementioned ones, the motion may be made at any time prior to the final disposition of the case.

25. How a Motion for Disqualification Should be Made and Its Procedure

A motion for disqualification may be made by a petition to the court or by making a declaration to the clerk of the court having him prepare a formal petition in that respect.

The moving party is obliged to offer proof of the grounds upon which disqualification is sought and a mere statement of belief is insufficient proof.

The court may require a judge whose disqualification is sought to comment on the particulars which furnish the basis of the motion, and the judge must set forth his conclusions as to the sufficiency of these particulars.

26. Disposition of Motions for Disqualification of Judges

The motion to disqualify a judge is decided by that court of which the challenged judge is a member. However, if the non-participation of the challenged judge results in the court's lacking a sufficient quorum and the court is a court of first instance, the

Aggravated Felony Court in the same jurisdiction shall decide on the matter and, if the disqualification of the judge of an Aggravated Felony Court is demanded, then the next nearest Aggravated Felony Court shall hear and decide the motion.

If the motion for disqualification is directed against a justice of the peace or an investigating judge, the motion is decided by the appropriate court of first instance, or if the aforesaid motion is directed against a single judge in a single judge court, the Aggravated Felony Court in the same jurisdiction hears and decides the motion. Nevertheless, if the judge who is sought to be disqualified accepts the motion, no further decision on disqualifications is required.

Where the motion for disqualification is rejected for insufficiency of the grounds, the deciding authority shall impose upon the mover a light fine of not less than 10 nor more than 200 Lira. If the grounds upon which the motion was urged are proven false, the fine may not be less than 50 Lira.

The imposition of a fine shall not prejudice the rights of a judge to pursue his legal remedy against the person making an unfounded motion for disqualification, or to present a criminal prosecution or the rights of the Public Prosecutor to criminally prosecute the maker of an unfounded motion for disqualification.

27. Decisions on Motions for Disqualification and Interlocutory Appeal

Decisions granting motions for disqualification are final. Where the motion is summarily denied, an independent urgent exception against the decision may be taken. Where the motion is denied for insufficiency of the grounds, the interlocutory appeal can only be made as part of the appeal after verdict.

28. Competency of a Challenged Judge

A judge who is the subject of a motion to disqualify may, until the motion is decided, discharge only those functions necessary to prevent a prejudicial delay in the proceedings.

29. Transfer of Proceedings When Judge Disqualifies Himself

Where a judge disqualifies himself on his own motion, the authority charged with considering the challenge may give the case to another judge or transfer it to another court.

Where there is doubt concerning the impartiality of a judge, the authority charged with reviewing the case can also decide this matter on its own motion.

30. Disqualification of Court Clerks

The provisions of this Chapter shall apply also to the clerks of the various courts herein covered.

CHAPTER 4

DECISIONS, PRONOUNCEMENT AND NOTIFICATION

31. When the Decision is Given

In cases requiring a hearing, the decision is rendered after hearing the parties to the dispute. In cases which do not require a hearing, the decision is rendered after the oral or written submissions of the Public Prosecutor are taken.

32. Decisions Requiring Written Opinions

Decisions from which an appeal is permitted and decisions refusing an application for particular relief ought to include the reasons therefor.

33. Pronouncement and Notice of Decisions

Where the interested party is present, the decision is orally delivered in his presence, and if he so requests, he shall be furnished with a written copy of the decision.

Notice of other decisions is given to the parties.

Where the interested party is under arrest, all notified documents are read and explained to him upon his request.

34. Decisions to be Forwarded to the Public Prosecutor; Performance and Execution of Notifications and Decisions

Judgments and decisions to be given notice of and executed are forwarded to the Public Prosecutor. The Public Prosecutor is responsible for the giving of notice and execution of such judgments and decisions.

This provision does not apply to internal administrative proceedings of the courts and to interlocutory disciplinary measures.

Investigating Judges and Justices of the Peace have authority to perform and execute all types of notifications and decisions.

35. Notice

The appropriate provisions of the Code of Civil Procedure concerning notice shall also apply to criminal matters.

36. Calling Witnesses and Securing Expert Testimony by the Interested Party

A party to a criminal action who is entitled directly to call witnesses and offer expert testimony applies through the clerk of the court to have such witnesses called.

37. Substituted Service

Where it has been impossible to obtain personal service of the summons on the accused who is within Turkey, or where the accused is outside of Turkey and it appears that personal service of the summons according to statutory provisions would be impossible or would be futile, publication of the summons notice in a Turkish or foreign newspaper shall constitute legal notice to the accused and shall be perfected after the passing of two weeks from the date of publication, OR, in the alternative, posting of the warrant in the Court House shall also constitute legal notice to the accused in these circumstances.

Selection of the newspaper in which publication is to be made lies within the discretion of the authority charged with the duty of giving notice.

If supplementary service of notice is required on a person already duly served with a summons and it appears that it is impossible to obtain personal service of such supplementary notice within Turkey, such supplementary notice may be made by posting for two weeks the appropriate papers giving notice in the Court House.

This constitutes a legal notice.

Where it is necessary to serve notice of the decision and the sentence and it is necessary to resort to substituted service in accordance with the above paragraph, it shall be sufficient to post only the decision of the court in the Court House.

38. Notification to Public Prosecutor

The Public Prosecutor is given notice of the contents of papers by exhibition of the originals. If such notification shall have the effect of commencing the running of a time limitation, the Public Prosecutor shall record upon such document the date upon which it was exhibited to him.

Chapter 5

LIMITATIONS OF TIME AND REINSTATEMENT

39. Limitation Measured by Days

Where a limitation period is measured according to days, the actual day of the notification or of occurrence of the incident used to describe the beginning of the period shall not be considered.

40. Limitations Measured by Weeks or Months

Where the period is stated in terms of weeks, it shall expire at the time of office closing hours on the same day of the latest week. Where the period is stated in months, it shall expire at the time of the office closing hours on the same numbered day of the latest month and if there is no equivalent day in the latest month, then, on the last day of that month.

Where the last day of a period falls on a Sunday or holiday, the term shall expire on the day following.

Where a person subject to a time limitation resides in a place so remote from the place of proceeding that the imposition of the time limitations would be unreasonable, the provisions of Article 164 of the Code of Civil Procedure shall apply.

41. Inability to Comply with Limitations of Time

Where, because of force majeur, or because of unexpected and unavoidable circumstances, it is impossible for a party to comply with a limitation of time, such a party may petition the court to waive the defect and to reinstate the parties into the original status quo. Ignorance of the existence of a notice, if not due to personal fault, constitutes an unexpected and unavoidable circumstance.

42. Submission of the Petition of Reinstatement

The petition of reinstatement should be filed during the week following the ending of the cause of inability to comply with the time limitation. The petition must be filed with the court which

27

would have taken the procedural steps in case of compliance with the limitation.

In his petition, the applicant shall state the reasons for his failure to comply and submit proof of the circumstances giving rise to his failure. At that time he shall undertake whatever other procedural steps he has failed to take.

43. To Whom Plea is Made and Effect of Ruling

If the time limitation has been complied with, the court having jurisdiction of the proceedings shall consider the petition of reinstatement.

The decision of the court on such a petition is final. An urgent exception, however, may be taken against the decision of rejection of the request for reinstatement.

44. The Effect of the Petition of Reinstatement on the Decision

A petition of waiver regarding a failure to comply with a time limitation shall not postpone the execution of a decision. However, the court may nevertheless suspend execution of the judgment.

CHAPTER 6

WITNESSES

45. Summoning Witnesses

Witnesses are invited to court by summons. The consequences of a failure to appear shall be set forth in the summons.

In urgent cases where the accused is detained, either a court or an investigating judge may issue a subpoena to a witness outside its area of jurisdiction, giving prior notice to such persons. Witnesses who appear upon subpoena shall not be treated differently from witnesses who appear voluntarily upon a notice given by the investigating judge.

Summonses to military personnel on active duty shall be served by the military authorities.

46. Failure of Witnesses to Appear

Witnesses who fail to appear after having appropriately been summoned are subject to a light fine not exceeding 10 Lira and are liable for any damages resulting from their failure to appear. Such fine shall be converted to imprisonment if it is not paid. In such case the witness may be brought before the court by force upon issuance of a subpoena.

In the event that no order for arrest is made but a second summons is issued, the witness may be twice punished if he fails to respond to the second summons.

If the witness fails to appear by reason of justifiable excuse, he is not subject to punishment. If an order has been made for his punishment, it shall be withdrawn upon the showing of the facts constituting the basis of the excuse.

Persons having authority to take witnesses' depositions outside the jurisdiction of the court entertaining the case, and both investigating judges and justices of the peace during preliminary investigations, are authorized to act in accordance with the preceding paragraphs.

With respect to military personnel on active duty, a subpoena to appear shall be served by the military authorities.

47. Persons Exempted from Testifying

The following persons may refuse to testify:

(1) The fiancée of the accused.

(2) Any person who is or has been the husband or wife of the accused.

(3) Persons related to the accused in the direct line, whether by blood relationship or affinity relationship, persons collaterally related to the accused within three degrees; persons collaterally related to the accused by a present or previously dissolved marriage within two degrees; and persons having a relationship to the accused by virtue of adoption.

The aforementioned persons shall be given notice of their privilege before being called upon to testify. Any of the aforementioned persons may assert his privilege at any stage of his testimony regardless of whether he has previously withdrawn his right to assert such privilege.

48. Professional Privilege

Lawyers, physicians and midwives may refuse to testify concerning matters of which they have knowledge as a result of their professional status. However, where the person concerned with such matters agrees to the admission of testimony concerning such matters, the privilege may not be asserted.

49. Testimony Concerning State Secrets

Unless the permission of the responsible official is first obtained, government employees and officers are forbidden to testify concerning information acquired as a result of their official duties and which they are obliged to conceal, even after the termination of their service or employment.

In such cases, for a member of the Council of Ministers, the permission of the president, and for a member of the Grand National Assembly, the permission of the Grand National Assembly is required.

When permission to testify is requested, it may be given unless such testimony would be harmful to interests of the State.

The President of the Republic judges for himself the secrecy of the matter and may refuse to testify.

The above rule applies also to former presidents and the information acquired by them during their previous terms of office.

50. Refusal to Testify Against One's Self or Against One's Dependants or Family

A witness can refuse to testify where such testimony can incriminate him or any of his relatives named in paragraphs 1, 2 or 3 of Article 47.

51. Assertion of Privilege—Reasons

In order to assert the privileges recognized by Articles 47, 48 and 50, the witness must assert the privilege and, when requested, state the particular grounds upon which the privilege is asserted, and this must be done under oath.

52. Witnesses Disabled from Testifying Under Oath

The following persons shall testify without oath:

(1) Persons who have not achieved the age of fifteen years at the date of testimony or who, because of weakness of mind, have insufficient comprehension of the meaning and nature of the oath.

(2) Persons prohibited from public service while serving a sentence for conviction of a crime.

(3) Persons who have participated in or abetted the activities which are the subject of a prosecution.

53. Testimony of Witnesses Who Decline to Assert Privilege

The judge shall decide whether or not it is necessary to confirm by oath the testimony of a witness who is privileged according to Article 47 but who has declined to assert the privilege. Nevertheless, any privileged witness can refuse to testify under oath and he should be informed of this right.

54. Examination of Witnesses

Every witness shall be examined separately and consecutively and no witness shall be examined in the presence of another.

Until the opening of the final investigation, witnesses shall associate neither with one another nor with the accused, except where such isolation will cause prejudicial delay and except in making identifications.

55. Advising the Witness of the Gravity of His Function

Where the judge finds it necessary he shall explain to the witness before he is sworn the significance and importance of what he is to be called upon to do.

56. Swearing of Witnesses

Each witness shall be sworn separately before testifying. However, where necessary or where there appears doubt as to whether the testimony of a person is permissible, the oath of the witness may be postponed until after the testimony has been received.

57. Form of Oaths

The witness shall be required to give the following oath before testifying:

" I promise upon my honor and my conscience to disclose what I know of the truth without concealing anything, without adding anything, without fear of any person, and without influence of any type whatsoever."

After testifying, the witness shall be required to give the following oath:

" Without concealing anything, without adding anything, fearing no one, and without influence of any type whatsoever, I promise upon my honor and my conscience that I have disclosed what I know of the truth."

During the administering of the oaths, everyone shall stand.

58. Taking the Oath—Provisions for Dumb Persons

Ordinarily a witness makes his oath by repeating the oath in a loud voice or by reading it in a loud voice.

Dumb persons who can neither read nor write shall swear their oaths by making appropriate motions with their heads and their hands and through the medium of a third person capable of interpreting the significance of such motions. Dumb persons who can write shall make their oaths by writing out the oath and signing it.

59. Swearing of Witnesses During Preparatory Investigations

Witnesses cannot be required to give oaths during the preparatory investigation. Nevertheless, in cases where the absence of sworn testimony is likely to result in prejudicial delay or cases of flagrant offenses, the Public Prosecutors, Justices of the Peace, or Investigating Judges can swear a witness.

This article may be invoked where it is necessary to obtain testimony on a fact which has been made in the preparation of the accusation of the Public Prosecutor.

The reason for requiring an oath in these circumstances shall be made a part of the record.

60. Subsequent Testimony of a Witness

Where it is necessary to recall during the same proceeding a witness previously sworn in that proceeding, such a witness need not take a new oath, it being sufficient if he is reminded of his original oath and advised that the subsequent testimony is subject thereto.

61. Preliminary Questions to be Asked of the Witness

Before testifying, a witness shall be required to state his name, age, work or profession, religion and place of residence. Where necessary, further questions may be put concerning matters which may assist the judge in weighing the credibility of the witness, and questions may also be put dealing with the relations of the witness with the accused or injured person.

62. Instructing Witnesses and Permissible Questions

The judge shall explain to the witness the nature of the charge and, if the accused is present, identify him to the witness. Thereafter, the witness is requested to tell all he knows of the facts concerning the offense. The witness shall not be interrupted during his explanations.

Witnesses may be asked questions necessary to give a complete and coherent narrative and to elicit facts pertinent to the circumstances of the case.

63. Refusal to Testify or to Take an Oath Without Legal Grounds

A witness who refuses to testify or to take an oath without legal grounds for such a refusal is subject to damages in accordance with Article 46 of this code and to a fine. If the fine is not paid, it will be converted to an appropriate period of imprisonment.

In addition, while the action is pending and in order to compel necessary testimony and oath, a witness who refuses to take the oath and refuses to testify without legal cause may be imprisoned up to the time final judgment is given, but not more than six months.

However, in the case of a minor offense, the period of such confinement may not exceed six weeks.

Persons authorized to take depositions in places beyond the jurisdiction of the court, investigating judges, and justices of the peace during the preliminary investigation period, also have authority to invoke these provisions.

A witness shall be subject to these provisions only once during the pendency of the original action, or a related action.

64. Reimbursement of Witnesses

A witness summoned by a judge or the Public Prosecutor has the right to be reimbursed in an amount proportional to the time the witness has spent. He shall be reimbursed from State funds. Where the witness has been required to travel from a distant place, he is entitled to the cost of travel as well as the cost of maintaining himself in the place where the court is entertaining proceedings.

CHAPTER 7

INQUIRIES AND EXPERTS

65. Provisions Applicable to Experts

Except as hereinafter provided, the provisions of Chapter 6 shall apply to experts called upon to testify in court.

66. Appointment of Experts

The number of experts required for any proceeding and the appointment of such experts are matters within the power and discretion of the judge.

Nevertheless, if delay is detrimental, the Public Prosecutor shall have authority to appoint experts for the purposes of preliminary proceedings.

Where official experts, designated as those obliged to give opinions, are available, no other experts shall be employed, except under special circumstances.

During preliminary proceedings, physical examinations may be made upon order of the Public Prosecutor.

67. Challenging Experts

Experts can be challenged on the same grounds permitting the challenge of a judge.

The fact that a person has testified as a witness in the same action does not disqualify such person from acting as an expert. The Public Prosecutor, complainant and accused have the right to challenge experts. Where experts are appointed by the court, those having the right to challenge them shall be notified of such right by the appointing judge, unless extraordinary conditions prevent it.

68. Persons Obliged to Give Expert Testimony

Persons officially designated as obliged to give opinions and conclusions on certain matters, or persons engaged in science or the arts where the testimony of such persons is necessary to the proper disposition of proceedings or who are officially licensed

35

to engage in such science or arts are obliged to give expert testimony when they are appointed by the court as expert witnesses.

Persons who at any time have manifested to the Ministry of Justice their willingness to give expert testimony are obliged to act as experts whenever so requested.

Where expert testimony is required for the purpose of establishing facts and circumstances, the same provisions applicable to witnesses shall apply to such experts.

69. Right to Decline; Persons Not Qualified as Experts

An expert may decline to testify for any of the reasons which allow a witness to decline. An expert may also be excused from giving opinion evidence on other grounds, provided they are acceptable to the court.

Government officials shall not be heard as experts, where it is declared that such testimony would be contrary to the obligations of official duty.

70. Unco-operative Experts—Sanctions

Where an expert has been duly summoned and is obliged to offer testimony but does not respond, or refuses to testify or to take an oath, he shall be liable for whatever damages his actions may cause and in addition, is subject to a light fine not to exceed 20 Lira.

Where the fine is not paid, the expert may be sentenced to an equivalent term in prison.

Where an expert repeatedly fails to respond, or repeatedly declines to take the oath or to give testimony, he shall be fined or imprisoned, in accordance with the above conditions, for each instance of defiance.

71. Judicial Examination of Experts

The judge may order and conduct the examination of an expert whenever, in his discretion, he deems it necessary.

72. Oaths of Experts

Before testifying or submitting his report, the expert shall swear that he will give his opinion impartially and according to knowledge and science.

Where the expert has previously taken an oath on the same general subject whereon his opinion is sought, it is not necessary for him to be resworn so long as he certifies that he understands that his new testimony is subject to the conditions of his previous oath.

73. Powers of Experts

Where the expert certifies it necessary for the preparation of his report or testimony, the proceedings may be turned directly to the hearing of witnesses and the interrogation of the accused. Accordingly, the expert shall be allowed access to the record, whether in part or entirely, and the expert shall be allowed to be present during the examination of witnesses and the interrogation of the accused and shall also be allowed to put questions directly, either to the accused or to the witnesses in the proceedings.

74. Mental Examinations

Where an expert has requested that the accused be given a mental examination, during the preparatory and preliminary investigation period, the investigation judge and, where proceedings are in a more advanced stage, the court may order the accused to be placed under examination in an official institution upon hearing both the accused and the Public Prosecutor with respect to such a request.

Where the accused has no counsel, a counsel may be appointed for him by the court.

The accused may lodge a summary protest against the decision to confine him in an institution for observation. Such a protest, when made, shall arrest the execution of the decision.

The accused may not be detained for examination in an official institution for a period longer than six weeks.

75. Rendering of Opinions

During preliminary proceedings, including the initial investigation, experts' opinions are submitted in written form. With respect to ordinary matters, however, an oral opinion shall be sufficient provided it is made a part of the record and duly certified by the expert.

76. Defective Reports of Experts

If in the opinion of the judge the expert's report is inadequate or defective, he may order the expert to submit a new report or appoint a new expert for that purpose.

If, following the submission of his report, disqualification of the expert is successfully sought, the judge may appoint a new expert for the purpose of submitting a new report.

Where necessary, the advice of specialized official government departments may be sought.

77. Compensating Experts

In addition to compensation for loss of professional time, the expert shall receive, according to a fixed schedule, remuneration for his other investigatory and travel expenses sufficient for his work.

78. Investigations and Inquiries

Investigations and inquiries may be made by the judge, the judge's duly authorized agent, persons certified to take depositions in distant places, and in those instances where it may be necessary to obviate a prejudicial delay, by the Public Prosecutor.

When an investigation or inquiry is made, a report should be kept to state existing facts and conditions and the absence of traces and marks which ought to be expected, and this report should be incorporated into the record.

79. Autopsies and Examination of Corpses

Official examination of a corpse must be made in the presence of a physician. An autopsy shall be performed in the presence of a judge and in those cases where it is necessary to avoid prejudicial delay, the autopsy shall be performed by two physicians in the presence of the Public Prosecutor, at least one of the physicians being a forensic practitioner.

In an emergency situation, the operation may be conducted by one doctor only.

The physician who treated the deceased during the last illness of the deceased is forbidden to perform the operation, although this physician may be invited to attend the autopsy in order to provide pertinent information regarding details of the deceased's illness and condition.

Where it is necessary to exhume a corpse for the purposes of examination or autopsy, permission may be had to do so.

80. Identification of Deceased Persons

Wherever possible, identification of the deceased should always be made by exhibiting the corpse to those persons acquainted with the deceased and having personal knowledge of him. Where a person has been accused of a crime in connection with this death, the body is also exhibited to the accused for purposes of identification.

81. Autopsy (Post-Mortem Examinations)

Where the circumstances of death appear to require an autopsy, such autopsy shall definitely consist of an opening of the head, chest and abdomen.

82. Examination of Body of Newly Born Child

The technical investigation to be made when performing an autopsy on the corpse of a newly born child shall mainly concern whether the child lived during or after delivery, whether it was born at the customary time, or, if premature, whether it was in a condition to live at the time of birth.

83. Procedures in the Event of Suspicion of Poisoning

In circumstances giving rise to suspicion of poisoning, the suspected substances removed from the corpse or found in other places shall be analysed by a chemist or by an appropriate authority officially assigned to such matters.

The judge may order this examination to be conducted by a forensic practitioner.

84. Investigation of Suspected Counterfeiting

Where necessary, coins and notes seized during forgery and counterfeiting proceedings shall be examined by those authorities having responsibility for the circulation of the original materials. These authorities shall state their opinions as to the method and manner of the forgery or counterfeiting operations and the consequences resulting from such operations.

With respect to the counterfeiting of foreign coins or currencies, the opinions of the appropriate Turkish officials shall be taken with respect to such matters.

85. Examination of Documents

In order to determine the authenticity or forgery of suspected documents, or in order to determine the identity of the suspected counterfeiter, a handwriting and seals analysis may be made by an expert.

CHAPTER 8

SEARCHES AND SEIZURES

86. Seizure and Custody of Evidentiary Materials

Materials likely to be useful as evidence in the investigation, or which are subject to seizure, are retained separately from other materials or secured in any other way.

If these materials are in the possession of a person who refuses to relinquish them upon proper demand, they may be forcibly taken.

87. Refusal to Relinquish Necessary Materials—Sanctions

A person in possession of such materials described in the preceding article shall be required to show or surrender the materials upon appropriate demand.

In instances where such surrender is refused, the imprisonment provisions of Article 63 are applicable to the person in possession of such materials.

The provisions of this article shall not apply to those persons otherwise entitled to refrain from giving testimony.

88. Materials Immune from Seizure

Where the highest official of a particular department certifies that divulging the contents of materials preserved by that particular department would be prejudicial to the safety of the State, such materials may not be required to be produced. If the certification appears unfounded, appeal may be made to the Ministry having jurisdiction over the particular department.

89. Personal Communications Immune from Seizure

Communications between the accused and those persons capable of asserting a privilege in accordance with the provisions of Articles 47 and 48 may not be seized so long as such communications are in the possession of persons having the right to assert the privilege, unless such persons participated in the events which are

41

the subject of the investigation and are not charged as being accomplices.

90. Authorizing Seizures

The judge shall have authority to authorize particular seizures. Nevertheless, in instances where it appears that injury will otherwise result, Public Prosecutors and Assistant Police Officers assigned to discharge the orders of the Public Prosecutors may make seizures.

Where a seizure is made without a decision of a judge and the person or adult relative thereof is not present at the time or place of seizure, or if, being present, such person or adult relative thereof openly protested against the seizure, the official making the seizure is required to obtain judicial confirmation of the seizure within three days of the time of seizure.

The possessor of the materials which have been the subject of seizure may apply to a judge, at any time, for a review of the legality of the seizure.

Authority to review the legality of a particular seizure rests with the Justice of the Peace of the area in which the seizure took place where an actual prosecution has not been begun. Where the seizure is made by the Public Prosecutor or subordinate police officials subsequent to a prosecution, the judge exercising jurisdiction over the proceedings is notified within three days of the seizure and the materials seized are made available for his use.

In places assigned for military services, including warships, the seizure shall be made by the appropriate military authorities upon the request of and with the participation of the judge or the Public Prosecutor.

Nevertheless, the intervention of the military authorities is not required if such places are actually occupied or under the exclusive control of persons having no connection with the military authorities.

91. Seizure of Letters, Telegrams and Other Communications Addressed to the Accused

Seizure at the Post Office of letters, telegrams and other communications addressed to the accused is permissible.

Letters and other communications sent by the accused or letters and communications believed to be destined for the accused, although not addressed to him, if there are any facts reasonably supporting such belief, may also be seized provided that it is established that the contents of these letters bear upon the investigation being made of the accused.

92. Authorization for Seizure of Letters, Telegrams and Other Communications

Seizures mentioned in the foregoing article may be made only by a judge.

In instances other than petty offenses, where it appears that prejudicial delay may otherwise result, such seizures may also be made by the Public Prosecutor.

In such instances where the Public Prosecutor acts, he is obliged to surrender the seized material to the judge, and particularly letters and other postal communications, without opening them.

Seizures by Public Prosecutors shall be null and void, even where the seized materials are not yet in the custody of the Public Prosecutor, unless the order for seizure is certified by a judge within three days of the making of the order.

The judge entertaining jurisdiction in accordance with the procedure of Article 90 shall decide the validity of a seizure ordered by a Public Prosecutor and determine whether or not letters and other postal communications are to be opened.

93. Notice Following Postal Seizures

Except where delay prejudicial to the investigation might result, the parties concerned shall be notified whenever the measures sanctioned by Sections 91 and 92 are taken.

Letters and other communications seized shall be immediately delivered to the appropriate persons if no decision has been given to open them. The same procedure applies to those letters and communications which have been opened but found unnecessary to retain in custody.

Where a letter is retained, copies of those parts of the letter not pertinent to the investigation are forwarded to the addressee.

94. Searching Premises and Goods Belonging to the Accused, Accomplices of the Accused, and Receivers of Stolen Property

Premises, including the home, the goods and chattels as well as the physical person of a suspect, the accomplices of a suspect, or a person receiving stolen property may be searched.

Such searches may be made for the purpose of making an arrest, or where there are grounds to believe that necessary evidence may be discovered.

95. Searching Premises and Goods Belonging to Persons Other than the Accused, Accomplices or Receivers

Searches of persons other than those described in Article 94 may only be made at the houses or other premises of such persons and may only be made for the purpose of securing information or evidence for arresting the accused, to secure evidence as to the commission of an offense, or for the seizure of certain property.

In order for such searches to be made, however, there must exist facts inferring that the person sought, the evidence required, or the property subject to seizure is actually in the possession and control of the person against whom the search is to be made.

However, this restriction does not apply to such premises or places where the accused may be apprehended, through which he may have passed during pursuit, or which are under the supervision of the Public Security Administration.

96. Night Searches

Except where there is likely to be prejudicial delay or in flagrant offenses, or where it is necessary to recapture a detained or imprisoned person, night searches cannot be made in homes, working places or other premises closed to the public during that period.

This restriction does not apply to places occupied by persons under the special supervision of the Public Security Administration, to places which are open to the public at night, or to places where the accused persons may have retired or taken refuge or secreted stolen property. Nor does the restriction of this article apply to clandestine places of gambling nor to places of prostitution.

(N.B.—Last paragraph repealed and superseded by Kanunu, #6123 which amended certain articles of Turkish Penal Code.)

97. Authority to Order Searches

Authority to order searches and seizures rests with the judge. However, where there is a threat of prejudicial delay, public prosecutors and police officials charged with assisting the public prosecutors may also authorize a search.

In order to conduct a search of homes, working establishments, or other non-public places without the presence of a judge or a public prosecutor, it is necessary to have two persons from the village council or two neighbors present during the search.

The restriction set forth in the foregoing paragraph shall not apply to those places set forth in paragraph 2 of Article 96.

Procedure as to searches in places assigned to military services, including warships, upon the request of the judge or the public prosecutor, as the case may be, shall be made forthwith by military authorities. Nevertheless, where the area in question is solely occupied by persons not officially connected with the military it is unnecessary to invoke the intervention of the military authorities.

98. Persons Present During Searches

The owner of the premises or the possessor of the goods subject to search may be present during the search. Where such person cannot be present, his representative, his adult relative, a person residing with him, or his neighbor may be present.

In such instances as are described in paragraph 1 of Article 95, the possessor or, in the event of his absence, the person designated to represent him for those purposes, shall be notified of the impending search and the purpose thereof.

The foregoing provision shall not apply to the possessors of premises described in paragraph 2 of Article 95.

99. Notice to Person Subject to Search

Upon his request, the person whose goods, premises or body has been subject to search shall be furnished with a written notice after the search has been completed, stating the purposes of the search in accordance with Articles 94 and 95 and the suspected unlawful act in accordance with Article 94. Moreover, upon his request, a person whose property has been seized shall be furnished with a written inventory of the goods seized or taken into custody, and, if nothing relevant is discovered, a notice to that effect shall be given to him.

100. Provisional Seizure

Where the goods found bear no relation to the suspected crime under investigation but upon examination give evidence of another and independent crime, such goods shall be retained under a provisional seizure and the facts forwarded to the public prosecutor.

101. Inventories of Goods Seized and Sealing Thereof

A complete inventory of goods surrendered or seized shall be made in each case, and such goods shall be officially sealed or marked in order to avoid any confusion, loss or damage to the goods.

102. Authority to Examine Papers and Documents

Authority to examine the papers and documents of a person who is the subject of a search order rests with the judge. Other officials may examine such matters only with the consent of the possessor. If the possessor of the papers or documents refuses to consent to an examination by such lesser official, the official shall, where possible, and in the presence of the possessor, place such documents and papers in an envelope, seal the envelope and forward such envelope to the judge.

The possessor of the papers and documents, or his representative, may also affix his seal to the envelope. Where it is subsequently decided to examine the contents of any such envelope so forwarded, the possessor of the documents or his representative, if possible, is invited to be present when the seal is broken and such examination made. The judge shall transmit such papers bearing on the crime as he shall discover to the Public Prosecutor.

103. Restoring Property of the Victim Held for Evidentiary Purposes

Property taken from the victim of a crime shall be summarily returned to him at a time no later than the end of the investigation without the necessity of a formal order or decision, unless there is a third party protest.

Concerned parties shall not forfeit their rights to bring a civil action to recover damages for any unlawful withholding of property.

ARREST, PROVISIONAL DETENTION AND RELEASE

104. Circumstances Requiring Arrest

A person may be arrested where there is great suspicion connecting him with a particular crime, under the following circumstances:

(1) Where there are facts indicating that the person suspected plans to make an escape.

(2) Where there are facts indicating that the person is attempting to remove evidence or traces of criminal activities, or encouraging his accomplices or witnesses to make false statements or to refuse to testify.

(3) Where the offense of which the person is suspected is against public morals, against the security of the public, or is against the authority of the State or the government.

The existence of such facts shall be recited in the decision of arrest.

In the following instances the suspect shall always be presumed to be planning to make an escape:

(1) Where the offense of which the person is suspected is a felony.

(2) Where the suspect has no domicile or residence, is a vagrant, a suspicious character, or unable to identify himself.

(3) Where the suspect is a foreigner and there are strong indications that he would neither respond to a summons nor surrender for the execution of the judgment.

105. Arrest for Minor Offenses

Where the crime is a lesser offense the suspect may be arrested only if he falls within the categories set forth in numbers 2 and 3 of paragraph 2 of Article 104, if he is expected to escape, or if he is a person subject to police supervision.

106. Arrest Procedure—Form of Warrant

The arrest of a suspect is accomplished by a warrant of arrest issued by the judge.

The warrant shall contain a description and identification of the suspect and shall describe the circumstances and the crime of which he is suspected, with clarity.

Notice is given at the time of arrest in accordance with Article 33 and, where this is impossible, notice of the crime for which a suspect has been arrested must be given him no later than the day following the day of his detention.

107. Notice of Arrest to Persons Other than the Accused

Where the making of the arrest will not be jeopardized, the arrested person may be permitted to notify his relatives or other persons with whom he is closely associated. Upon the request of the accused, these persons shall be given official notice of the arrest.

108. Examination of a Person Under Arrest

Where a person has been arrested pursuant to a warrant, he shall be, immediately and no later than the day following the day of his arrest, arraigned before the appropriate judge.

The judge shall, immediately and upon the next day following the arrest, examine the detained person with respect to those matters of which he is suspected. During the examination, the arrested person shall be advised of those facts which may be used against him.

The examination shall be conducted in such a manner as not to impair whatever evidence the accused may be able to put forward in his own behalf.

109. Release

Where the accused is not arraigned before the appropriate judge upon the day of his arrest he may, upon his request, be arraigned, immediately and upon the day of his arrest, before the nearest Justice of the Peace.

Paragraphs 2 and 3 of Article 108 shall also apply in these cases.

If the warrant of arrest is withdrawn during the examination or when it is established that the person held is not the person identified in the warrant, such person shall be released forthwith.

110. Withdrawal of the Warrant of Arrest

A person under arrest may petition the examining official for the withdrawal of the warrant of arrest, or for release in accordance with the provisions of Article 117.

After examining the petition, the examining official shall rule upon the request and notice of the decision shall be given to the accused and made a part of the investigation record.

111. Exception Taken by the Accused Against the Decision of Arrest

Where a petition by the accused made in accordance with the provisions of the previous article is rejected, the accused may, upon being given notice of the rejection, take exception against the rejection.

112. Review of Necessity of Detention

While under detention, the appropriate examining authority shall have plenary power to examine and to consider at regular intervals the expediency of a continued detention of the accused. Such an examination ought definitely to be made within thirty days from the date of the arrest of the accused.

Where the examining authority decides not to release the accused, he shall at the same time set another date for a review of the necessity of detention.

Such intermittent examinations shall be made at intervals of not less than three weeks nor more than two months.

Nevertheless, examinations may be made at more frequent intervals than those set forth in the preceding paragraph where request for such examination is made by the accused.

When the defendant makes timely objection to the decision of his arrest or against the decision rejecting his petition for release, or when a decision to open trial (final investigation) is coupled with an order of continuance of arrest, the period starts anew from the time of oral or written notice to the defendant concerning such order.

113. *Repealed.*

[Art. 2, Law #3006.]

114. *Repealed.*

[Art. 2, Law #3006.]

115. *Repealed.*

[Art. 2, Law #3006.]

116. Place of Detention and Treatment of the Detained Person

Whenever possible, a person who is detained before trial shall be detained separately from convicts and, where possible, in a separate enclosure. The extent of restriction shall be proportional to the requirements of the arrest with due regard to the requirement of maintaining order in the institution where the person is detained. The detained person may take whatever steps he desires to provide himself with rest and occupation in accordance with his wealth and social position during the term of his detention so long as such measures do not interfere with the peace and good order of the institution of detention and so long as such measures do not prejudice the purpose of the detention.

A person under detention may be put into chains only when he is a serious threat to the safety of the institution, or where it is thought necessary for the protection of the other prisoners, or where he has attempted to commit suicide, or where he has attempted to escape, or where he has made preparations for such activities.

A detained person shall not be brought to the hearing in chains.

The aforementioned extraordinary measures may be taken only upon the authority of a judge. In emergency situations, such extraordinary measures may be taken by other officials, but when so taken, the assent of the judge shall be sought at the earliest opportunity after they are taken.

117. Release on Bail

Except for the grounds stated in Section 2 of Paragraph 1 of Article 104, the accused shall be released upon the posting of appropriate bail.

Repeated offenders and persons for which an order of arrest is given according to the last paragraph of Article 200 of this Code shall not benefit from the privileges of this Article.

118. Form of Bail

Bail may be given in the form of money, government bonds, security, or the financial guaranty of a respectable person.

The amount and form of bail shall be determined by the judge.

119. Appointment of an Agent for Those not Residing in Turkey and Seeking Release

Where the accused does not reside in Turkey and seeks release in accordance with the provisions of the foregoing Articles, he shall appoint someone residing within the jurisdictional area of the court to answer for him and to receive notices directed to him.

120. Reapprehension of a Person Released on Bail

Where the accused who has been released on bail makes preparations for escape or, without legal excuse, fails to respond to a summons or warrant, or if new grounds are discovered requiring his detention, he shall be reapprehended notwithstanding the bail.

121. When No Bail Required—Return of Bail

After an accused is released on bail, the bail will be returned to him in case he is arrested for another crime, or if the warrant of arrest is withdrawn, or if he is punished with a sentence which limits the freedom, provided that the bail has not yet been forfeited.

Where the person furnishing bail secures the presence of the accused before the court on the date designated by the judge, or if he notifies the court of an intention on the part of the accused to escape so as to allow for rearrest of the accused, his bail shall be returned to him.

122. Forfeiture of Bail—Summary Protest against Forfeiture

If the accused does not appear during the investigation or escapes from the execution of a sentence which limits the freedom, bail posted on his behalf is forfeited to the Treasury. Before a decision on this matter is given, however, the person furnishing the bail for the accused shall be notified and allowed to be heard. Only a summary protest can be made against such a decision.

Before the court deals with the protest, those concerned with the matter and the Public Prosecutor shall be permitted to assert their claims orally and to submit evidence in support of such claims.

The decision ordering the forfeiture of bail shall nevertheless apply temporarily against the person furnishing bail during the period when appeal against such decision may be made.

When the prescribed period within which protest must be made has expired, the forfeiture of bail shall be considered final and accorded the finality of a judgment of a civil court.

123. Withdrawal and Expiration of Warrant of Arrest

The warrant of arrest shall expire and lose all legal effect where there is no foundation for an arrest and it has been decided that there are no grounds upon which the accused may be detained, or where the accused has been acquitted by the appropriate court.

Application for appeal shall not postpone the release of the accused.

124. Authority to Confirm Arrests or to Order Releases

Confirmation of arrests and orders releasing persons on bail are given by the appropriate judge.

Decisions of investigating judges denying Public Prosecutors' requests for inquiries where the accused persons are not taken into custody, decisions ordering arrests, decisions withdrawing warrants of arrest, decisions ordering release of detained persons on bail or otherwise, and decisions dismissing indictments, are all subject to confirmation by the presiding judge of the court of first instance in the particular area.

Where the Public Prosecutor desires the arrest of an accused, he shall request the appropriate authority to issue a warrant for such an arrest. The authority so requested is obliged to give a decision either accepting or rejecting the request.

In emergency instances, the president of the court up to and including the time of the decision as to the necessity of a final inquiry, or up until such time as the accused is actually brought to court under indictment, may also exercise such authority.

125. Warrants Issuable by Justices of the Peace

A Justice of the Peace may issue warrants of arrest upon the request of the Public Prosecutor showing good cause for arrest provided the public prosecution has not yet begun. A Justice of the Peace may also issue warrants of arrest on his own initiative where there is a threat of prejudicial delay.

The right to arrest persons or to order their release on bail belongs to the Justice of the Peace of that area where the crime is committed or where the accused is apprehended.

In such instances the provisions of Articles 106–123 are applicable.

126. Plea to Withdraw Warrant—Release of Accused by Public Prosecutor

Where the Public Prosecutor does not file a public prosecution, or where the Public Prosecutor deems the further detention of the accused unnecessary, the warrant of arrest shall expire and lose all legal effect. In such cases, the Public Prosecutor shall immediately release the accused.

127. Arrest in Cases of Flagrant Offenses

Where it is believed that a person, interrupted during the commission of a flagrant offense, or being pursued for a flagrant offense, will attempt to escape and it is impossible otherwise to identify such a person, he may be temporarily placed under arrest by anyone without the requirement of a warrant. In cases where a warrant of arrest should be issued, but the delay thereby caused would be detrimental, police officers may temporarily arrest the accused, if there is no possibility of an immediate plea to their superiors or to the Public Prosecutor.

When a flagrant offense which necessitates a complaint for inquiry is committed against minors, physically disabled persons, mentally disabled persons, or against any person not in full possession of his faculties, the apprehension and detention of the perpetrator of such an offense may be made without prior complaint and without warrant.

Flagrant offenses are crimes interrupted during their commission; crimes whose commission have immediately preceded observation; crimes committed by persons under pursuit of the police, the victim, or, where the crime has immediately preceded the pursuit, by any person; or crimes evidenced by the existence of stolen goods or other evidence inferring that a crime has taken place immediately before the apprehension of the perpetrator, where such goods or evidence are found on or with the person of the perpetrator.

128. Examination of Arrested Persons

In order to eliminate delay and preserve the rights of the accused, following arrest, he must either be released or brought before a Justice of the Peace. He is examined by the Justice of the Peace no later than one day following his arrest and detention.

Where the Justice of the Peace finds no grounds for arrest or grounds for arrest no longer exist because of intervening events, the Justice of the Peace shall order the immediate release of the accused.

Otherwise, the provisions of Article 126 shall apply to the warrant of arrest which he shall issue.

129. Arraignment of the Accused

When a formal prosecution has been opened, the arrested person, whether previously brought before a Justice of the Peace or not, shall be immediately arraigned before the appropriate court or investigating judge. When the arrested person has been detained pursuant to a ruling of a Justice of the Peace, this ruling is presented as part of the arraignment.

The court or the investigating judge must decide on his further detention or release no later than one day following the arraignment.

130. Crimes Requiring Informations or Complaints—Notice to Persons Entitled to Complain or File Informations

In cases of such crimes as ordinarily require a complaint, and when, according to the last paragraph of Article 127, the accused is apprehended before such complaint is filed, those persons entitled to file such complaints are given notice of the arrest.

The provisions of Article 126 shall apply also in such cases.

131. Warrant of Seizure—Grounds for Issuance

Where the person subject to arrest is fleeing arrest, or where he is concealing himself in order to avoid arrest, the Public Prosecutor, and in extraordinary cases the judge, may issue a warrant of seizure which is based on the prior authority of the warrant of arrest.

A warrant of seizure cannot be issued without a prior warrant of arrest except where the person against whom it is issued is an escaped convict or a person who has fled while being temporarily detained. In the foregoing instances subordinate police officials may also issue a warrant of seizure.

The warrant of seizure shall state, as far as possible, the identity of the accused, a description of the accused, the crime of which he is accused, and the place where he is to be sent.

The provisions of Articles 108 and 109 shall apply to those persons subject to the provisions of a warrant of seizure.

CHAPTER 10

INTERROGATION OF ACCUSED

132. Summoning the Accused for Questioning

In order to question the accused, he is summoned to appear. It may be stated in the summons that his failure to appear shall result in his being brought by force.

133. Subpoena

An accused may be subpoenaed where sufficient grounds exist for the issuance of a warrant of arrest.

The subpoena shall clearly identify the accused, describe him, set forth the type of offense, and state the reasons why it is necessary to employ force.

134. Detention and Questioning of One Subpoenaed

An accused subject to subpoena shall immediately, and in no instance later than twenty-four hours after his apprehension, be questioned by the judge, and he may be detained no longer than is required for such questioning.

135. Questioning Procedure

Before questioning shall begin, the accused must be advised of the nature of the charges against him and asked if he wishes to answer to such charges. Questioning shall not be directed toward weakening or discrediting any evidence which the accused may have or wish to marshall in his own defense. During the initial examination, knowledge concerning the identity and personal status of the accused shall also be acquired.

Chapter 11

DEFENSE PROCEDURE

136. Selection of Defense Counsel by the Accused

At any and every stage of the proceedings the accused shall have the right to seek the advice of, and be represented by, one or more counsel.

Where the accused is compelled to appear through a statutory representative, such representative shall have the right to select a counsel to act on behalf of the accused.

137. Defense Counsel

Defense counsel may be chosen from those persons having the right to act as advocates or solicitors.

138. Appointment of Defense Counsel by the Court

Where the accused is under the age of fifteen years, or where he is deaf or dumb, or where he is mentally or physically disabled to the degree that he is unable to defend himself, and he has not acquired counsel to represent him, the court may appoint counsel for him.

139. Termination of the Duty of Counsel Appointed by the Court

Where the accused who has had counsel appointed for him by the court subsequently selects his own counsel and such counsel agrees to act in this respect, the duties of the appointed counsel shall terminate forthwith.

140. Qualifications of Counsel Appointed by the Court

Counsel may be appointed by the judge only from those persons qualified to act as attorneys in the area in which the court is located.

141. Dereliction of the Appointed Defense Counsel

Where the counsel appointed for the defendant in accordance with the provisions of Article 138 does not appear at the hearings or trial, or prematurely withdraws from the case, or neglects his duty toward the defendant, the president of the court may immediately appoint new counsel. In such circumstances the court may order a postponement of proceedings.

Where the new counsel asserts that a postponement is necessary in order to adequately prepare a defense, the proceedings shall be postponed or adjourned. In such instances, where proceedings must be adjourned because of the default of the defense counsel originally appointed by the court, such defense counsel, in addition to being subject to disciplinary action by the court, shall be liable for whatever expenses and costs result from the postponement made necessary by his actions.

142. Appointment of Counsel to Represent More than One Accused

Where there is more than one defendant accused in the same action, one defense counsel shall be qualified to act for all and the court need not appoint more than one.

143. Examination of Record by Counsel

At the conclusion of the initial inquiry, or, if no inquiry is made preliminary to the indictment, at the conclusion of the indictment proceedings, defense counsel shall be accorded free access to examine all papers and documents pertinent to the case.

Where it is considered that no prejudicial harm may result, and that the purposes of the inquiries will not be jeopardized, defense counsel may be accorded access to the materials described in the foregoing paragraph even before those times set forth in that paragraph.

Defense counsel shall never be denied access to and examination of records reporting the examination of the accused, the reports of experts, and records of any legal proceedings the accused is entitled to attend.

Once the investigation record has been submitted to the court, defense counsel, even where there is more than one accused, shall be furnished a copy of this record without charge.

144. Rights to Confer with Counsel

A person under detention may at any time meet, confer with and correspond with his attorney.

Nevertheless, until the opening of the final investigation, if any, the judge may prohibit the disclosure of facts or other information unsuitable for the cognizance of the accused. Depending upon the nature of the charges and, where necessary, until the opening of the final investigation, the judge personally, or his duly appointed delegate, or a person designated by the judge to record, may be present during the meetings between the accused and his counsel.

145. Other Persons Qualified to be Present During the Proceedings and Qualified to Advise the Accused

Where the accused is a woman, her husband shall be entitled to act as her adviser, to be present at all proceedings, and to be heard, if he wishes, during the trial.

This provision is applicable to the statutory representatives of the accused. These persons may be admitted as advisers during the preliminary investigation upon the approval of the judge.

146. Fee of Appointed Counsel

Where defense counsel is appointed by the court, such defense counsel shall be awarded a fee in accordance with a previously adopted schedule, such fee to be paid by the State Treasury.

Where the accused is ultimately found guilty of the charges brought against him and sentenced, the State Treasury shall be entitled to recoup this amount from the accused.

Book II

PROCEDURAL REQUIREMENTS

CHAPTER 1

PUBLIC PROSECUTIONS

147. The Condition for Investigation

The preliminary and final investigation may only be started after a public prosecution is initiated.

148. Duty of Initiating Public Prosecutions

The duty of initiating public prosecutions lies with the Public Prosecutor.

Except as otherwise provided by law, the Public Prosecutor shall be required to initiate a public prosecution whenever there are circumstances and events which provide evidence, circumstantial or otherwise, requiring a prosecution.

A public prosecution may also be initiated by an order of the Minister of Justice directed to the Public Prosecutor.

A Provincial Governor may request the Public Prosecutor within the Provincial Governor's province to initiate a public prosecution. If the Public Prosecutor declines to act by submitting compelling reasons for this refusal, the Provincial Governor may, in the event of such a refusal, nevertheless request the Minister of Justice to order the initiation of the prosecution pursuant to the authority granted by this Article.

149. Discontinuance of Investigation Because of a New Crime —Renewal

When the accused is subject to punishment resulting from a crime unrelated to one for which he has previously been convicted and punished or will be punished, the prosecution may be discontinued.

Accordingly, the investigating judge, upon the request of the Public Prosecutor who had originally initiated the proceedings, may suspend the prosecution temporarily.

Where, however, the previous prosecution and conviction does not preclude a prosecution for a succeeding offense, the prosecution may be renewed.

Where, considering the punishment resulting from a conviction, a prosecution has been discontinued or postponed, the prosecution can be renewed only if the statute of limitations has not run during the intervening period, and must be renewed within three months from the final disposition of the other prosecution.

When a prosecution is renewed after a temporary suspension or discontinuance, a new indictment must be made.

150. Limitations on the Scope of Investigation and Power to Sentence

The punishment resulting from an investigation and conviction is determined by the crimes set forth in the indictment and can concern only those persons named in the indictment.

Within these limits the courts can act freely, but in applying the penal law the courts are not bound by the indictment.

CHAPTER 2

PREPARATION OF PUBLIC PROSECUTIONS

151. Reporting of Crimes

Crimes may be reported orally or in writing to Public Prosecutors, police officials, or Justices of the Peace.

Such reports may also be made to the legal authorities through governors (valiler), administrative chiefs of districts (kaymakamlar), or administrative chiefs of a sub-district (nahiye müdürleri).

Oral notices are reduced to writing.

For crimes where a complaint is necessary, a complaint, either written or verbal, may be made to the court or Public Prosecutor; if in written form, it may be made to the above-mentioned political authorities.

The terms " complaint " and " personal claim " used in the Penal Code have the same meaning and are subject to the same provisions.

152. Notification of Suspicious Death

Police and municipal officials or village aldermen are responsible for notifying the Public Prosecutor or the Justice of the Peace in any case where there is evidence that a death did not occur from normal causes, or where the corpse of an unknown person has been found.

Burial in such case can take place only upon written permission of the Public Prosecutor or the Justice of the Peace.

153. Duty of Public Prosecutor Informed of a Crime

As soon as he is informed of the occurrence of a crime, the Public Prosecutor is required to make necessary investigations for the purpose of deciding whether there is any necessity for the filing of a public prosecution.

The Public Prosecutor investigates evidence both against the accused and in his favor, and helps to preserve proof which otherwise might be lost.

65

154. Powers of Public Prosecutor

The Public Prosecutor may, for the purpose aforesaid, demand any information from any public employee. The Public Prosecutor is authorized to make his investigations either directly or through police officers. The police are obliged to execute orders of the prosecutor concerning legal procedures. Such orders are normally delivered in written form, but in emergency cases they may be given orally. When oral order in an emergency case is given, the Public Prosecutor informs the chief of police thereof.

Government employees who neglect or abuse their duties prescribed by law or required from them within the limits of the law, or police officers who neglect or disobey written or oral orders of the Public Prosecutor are subject to direct prosecution by the Public Prosecutor. However, chiefs of police are subject to the same procedures which are applied to judges; and valiler, kaymakamlar and nahiye müdürleri are subject to the Employees Procedure Law.

155. Demand of the Public Prosecutor for Investigation by Justice of the Peace

Where it is necessary that an investigation be conducted by a judge, the Public Prosecutor makes a demand upon the Justice of the Peace of the district where the alleged crime occurred. The Justice of the Peace determines whether prosecution is necessary in the light of the facts and the demand made.

156. Function of Police

Police officers are required to conduct investigations of crimes and to take such emergency measures as are necessary to clarify the facts. Such officers must send immediately to the Public Prosecutor the documents resulting from such investigations.

Where an investigation must be conducted immediately by a judge, however, such documents may be sent to the appropriate Justice of the Peace.

157. Obstruction of Investigation

An officer who has begun an investigation has the right to arrest any person who has obstructed him in the performance of his duties, and may keep such person under arrest until the completion of the investigation. However, the period of arrest may not exceed twenty-four hours.

158. Ex Officio Judicial Investigation

In cases where the accused is apprehended in the course of committing a crime, or where delay would be harmful, a Justice of the Peace has power *ex officio* to conduct all necessary investigations.

Public Prosecutors and investigating judges may also perform such procedures except for arrest.

159. Gathering Evidence in Favor of Accused

If, during the course of an inquiry conducted by the investigating judge or Justice of the Peace, the accused adduces evidence which indicates his innocence, such evidence shall be preserved if it is deemed acceptable by the judge, if the judge fears the disappearance of the evidence, and if the evidence necessitates the release of the accused.

When it appears necessary to secure such evidence within the jurisdictional area of a different court, an appropriate demand to that effect may be made to the examining judge or Justice of the Peace in that locality.

160. Authority of Public Prosecutor

The authority to continue the procedures in cases prescribed in Articles 158 and 159 rests with the Public Prosecutor.

161. Provisions to be Observed by the Investigating Judge, Justice of the Peace and Public Prosecutor During Preliminary Investigation

The formal execution of the preliminary investigation, to be conducted by the investigating judge or the Justice of the Peace, and participation of the court clerk, shall be in accordance with the procedures applicable to the initial inquiry.

Provisions of this article shall be observed by the Public Prosecutor in flagrant offenses or in cases where a delay is detrimental to protect the public interest.

162. Participation of Public Prosecutor

The Public Prosecutor acts together with the judge in accordance with the procedure applicable to initial inquiries.

These provisions apply also to those interrogated as suspects, those arrested, counsel selected by them, and to expert witnesses.

163. Opening of Public Prosecution

If preliminary investigation justifies the opening of a public prosecution, the Public Prosecutor institutes a case either by giving a written demand to the examining judge to open a preliminary investigation, or by making an accusation.

Otherwise, the Public Prosecutor decides that prosecution is not necessary and so informs the accused if he has testified earlier, or if a warrant of arrest has been issued against him.

164. Public Prosecutor's Decision Not to Prosecute

In cases where a private complaint is submitted to the Public Prosecutor, he informs the petitioner of the decision not to prosecute if he finds no reason for prosecution, or where he decides not to prosecute at the end of the preliminary investigation.

165. Objection to Such Decision

If the petitioner is, at the same time, the aggrieved, he may within fifteen days after notice, object to the Chief Justice of the nearest court which sees the Aggravated Felony cases and with which the Public Prosecutor is connected.

The objection must be accompanied by proof and facts which justify the opening of prosecution, and must be signed by a lawyer, if one has appeared on behalf of the petitioner.

166. Examination of Objection—Further Investigation

If the Chief Justice of the Aggravated Felony Court so demands, the Public Prosecutor sends him all documents prepared in connection with his investigation.

The court then notifies the accused, giving him an opportunity to be heard.

If, for rendering its decision, the court deems any further investigation necessary it appoints the investigating judge or Justice of the Peace to conduct it.

167. Refusal of Objection

If there is no cause to open a public prosecution, the court may refuse the petition, and if so, it informs the petitioner, the Public Prosecutor, and the accused.

After such action, a public prosecution may be opened only upon production of newly discovered evidence.

168. Acceptance of Objection

If the court is convinced that the petition is well founded and rightful, it orders opening of a public prosecution.

The Public Prosecutor executes this decision.

169. Security from Objector

Before rendering a decision on the petition, the court may demand from the petitioner the costs of petitioning and investigation as security for the treasury and the accused. Such security may be in the form of money or state bonds. The court determines the amount of security and the period within which the security is to be given.

If the security is not given within the prescribed period, the petition is deemed to have been withdrawn.

170. Costs of Objection

In cases provided in Articles 167–169, procedural costs are chargeable to the petitioner.

CHAPTER 3

PRELIMINARY INVESTIGATION

171. Cases in which Preliminary Investigation is Required

A preliminary investigation is required for serious felonies. In other cases, if the Public Prosecutor so desires, preliminary investigation may be made.

Preliminary investigation is not permitted for cases that will be tried by Justice of the Peace Courts, except where there is a joinder of such case with other cases within the jurisdiction of a higher court. If preparatory investigation has been conducted in accordance with Article 158 because of the flagrant offense or because a delay would be harmful, preliminary investigation is made by completing preparatory investigation.

172. Demand for Preliminary Investigation

A demand by the Public Prosecutor for a preliminary investigation shall specify the crime charged against the accused and his identity.

173. Refusal of Demand

Such demand may be refused on the ground that the court lacks jurisdiction; or that the public prosecution is not valid; or that preliminary investigation is not necessary for the type of crime charged; or that the charged offense is not punishable by the law.

The investigating judge decides such refusal. Before decision, the accused may be heard.

174. Opposition of the Accused to Opening of Preliminary Investigation

Upon notice to the Public Prosecutor, the accused may contest the decision on the opening of a preliminary investigation which should be pronounced according to Article 185, for any reason specified in the first paragraph of the previous Article.

The judge of the court of the first instance determines such opposition. The accused is notified of the decision in accordance with Article 185.

175. Accused's Protest

The accused may submit a petition of urgent exception against a decision of the chief justice of the court of first instance or of the examining judge overruling his objection made in accordance with the second paragraph of Article 173 and the first paragraph of Article 174.

In no other case can a separate proceeding be brought with respect to a decision of the chief justice or associate judge of the court of the first instance on the refusal of the objections made by the accused, or on the opening of a preliminary investigation.

176. Objections of Public Prosecutor and Accused

The Public Prosecutor may object to a decision refusing his demand for a preliminary investigation. The accused may also object to the gathering of evidence.

177. Conduct of Preliminary Investigation

A preliminary investigation is conducted by the investigating judge.

178. Other Officers Conducting Preliminary Investigation

A preliminary investigation may be assigned to a Justice of the Peace, upon the demand of the Public Prosecutor with the consent of the chief justice of the court of the first instance.

The investigating judge may demand a Justice of the Peace or an investigating judge of another jurisdiction to carry on part of the investigation.

When the Justice of the Peace has jurisdiction in the district of the investigating judge the previous provisions shall not apply.

179. Prosecution of Judges

Prosecutions of judges and persons who are so classified with respect to their duties and their personal crimes are conducted according to the Law on Judges.

180. Persons Who May be Present During Investigation

The investigating judge has present with him a recording clerk during the inquiry of the accused, the hearing of witnesses and experts, discovery and examination. In emergency cases, the investigating judge may designate a person to be recording clerk by administering an oath to him.

181. Record of Investigation

Each investigation is recorded. The record is signed by the investigating judge and by the recording clerk who was present.

The record contains the date and place of the investigation, the names of persons involved and of interested persons, and a notation as to whether essential procedural formalities have been complied with.

Those portions of the record which concern interested persons who have participated in the investigation are shown or read to them for ratification. Such ratification shall be included in the record, and interested parties shall sign it.

If they refuse to sign, the reasons for such refusal shall be stated.

182. Execution of Investigating Judge's Orders by Police

Police officers are required to execute orders and carry on inquiries ordered by the investigating judge.

183. What Preliminary Investigation Comprises

The preliminary investigation involves the gathering and preserving of evidence sufficient to decide whether there shall be an opening of a final investigation or a dismissal of the case.

Evidence that might be lost prior to the trial or evidence that is necessary to be obtained for the accused in the preparation of the defense must in any case be gathered.

184. Investigation Without Formal Order

During a preliminary investigation, if it is necessary to extend it to a person or a crime not included in the original demand, the investigating judge makes the necessary investigation without special order in emergency cases. In this case, the following necessary procedural steps shall be taken by the Public Prosecutor.

185. Re-Questioning of the Accused in the Preliminary Investigation

Even though the accused may have been questioned prior to the preliminary investigation, he may be questioned again in the preliminary investigation, and on this occasion, the decision on opening investigation shall be pronounced. The questioning may be done in the absence of the Public Prosecutor and counsel for the accused.

186. Persons Who May be Present During the Discovery and Examination and Hearing of Witnesses

The Public Prosecutor, the accused and his counsel may be present during the discovery and examination.

This provision shall apply also in the hearing of a witness or expert witness, where such a person is expected not to be present before the court during the trial or where it is deemed that his presence is difficult because of remoteness of his residence. Persons who are entitled to be present will be notified of delay in the proceedings.

If the accused is arrested he may only demand to be present at the proceedings in the courthouse where he is detained.

Those entitled to participation in the proceedings cannot obtain a postponement on personal grounds.

187. Presence of Accused

If the judge decides that the presence of the accused may prevent a witness from telling the truth, he may order the accused not to be present.

188. Right of Accused to Call Expert Witness

In case an examination by more than one expert witness is deemed necessary, the accused may request that the expert witness whom he intends to call during the trial be also cited to be present at such an examination. Where his request is rejected by the judge, the accused himself may invite the expert witness.

The expert witness invited by the accused is allowed to participate in the examination and investigation matters, provided, however, that he does not interfere with the duty of the expert witness appointed by the judge.

189. Examination of Documents by Public Prosecutor

The Public Prosecutor may at any time obtain information on the stage of investigation by examining the documents and may state accusations which he found as long as he does not delay the investigation.

190. Accomplishing the Purpose of the Investigation

As soon as the investigating judge is convinced that the purpose of the preliminary investigation has been accomplished, he turns over the documents to the Public Prosecutor so that he may present his case. If the demand of the Public Prosecutor is rejected by the investigation judge, he transfers the case to the chief or associate judge for his decision. This decision is final.

CHAPTER 4

DECISION AS TO COMMENCEMENT OF TRIAL *

191. Authority to Render Decision on Commencement or Suspension of Trial or Dismissal of Charges

The investigating judge is authorized to render a decision concerning the commencement of trial or temporary suspension thereof, or the dismissal of charges, in cases where a preliminary inquiry is necessary.

The Public Prosecutor files with the investigating judge the investigation documents together with his petition. The petition with respect to the commencement of a trial must be in the form of an accusation indicating clearly the charges.

192. Filing of Public Prosecution Where Preliminary Inquiry is Not Necessary

Where the Public Prosecutor files a public prosecution without a preliminary inquiry, he delivers the accusation together with the documents to the appropriate court.

193. Accusation

The accusation shall contain the following: the particulars of the offense attributed to the accused; the legal elements of the crime; the applicable statutory provision; the evidence, and the name of the court in which the trial will take place. For matters tried in a court of first instance, an Aggravated Felony Court, results of the preliminary criminal proceedings and the preliminary inquiry are also recorded in the accusation.

194. Notice to Accused

The investigating judge forwards a copy of the accusation and the decision concerning commencement of trial to the accused and asks him to state within three days whether or not he wishes to have more evidence obtained, or if he has any objection to the commencement of the trial.

* Final Investigation: Translator's note.

Any requirements and objections concerning these matters are decided by the investigating judge.

The accused may indicate his opposition to this decision in accordance with the provisions contained in the first paragraph of Article 173.

195. Decision for Further Clarification of the Problem and Decisions of the Judge of the Justice of the Peace Court

The investigating judge, either upon his own motion or upon the request of the Public Prosecutor or the accused, may render a decision extending the preliminary inquiry for the purpose of obtaining further clarifying evidence.

No objection against this decision is possible.

196. Decision for the Commencement of Trial

If at the end of the preliminary inquiry, sufficient cause exists to believe that the accused has committed the crime, the investigating judge renders a decision to commence the trial.

197. Decision to Dismiss the Charges

The investigating judge indicates the legal or the factual reasons upon which a decision to dismiss the charges is rendered.

198. Temporary Suspension of Trial

The investigating judge may temporarily suspend trial in the event that further proceedings become impossible because of the disappearance or mental unfitness of the accused to proceed.

199. Investigating Judge Not Limited by Accusation

The investigating judge is not bound by the accusation of the Public Prosecutor.

200. Decision on Commencement of Trial

In a decision by the investigating judge as to the commencement of trial, the nature of the crime imputed; its legal elements; the articles to be applied; and the appropriate court will be indicated. The investigating judge may order on his own motion the arrest of the accused or the continuation of arrest if he deems it necessary.

201. Public Prosecutor's Obligation to Conform to the Decision on Commencement of Trial and Invitation of the Accused

In the event that the Public Prosecutor asks for dismissal of the charges and the investigating judge orders commencement of trial, the Public Prosecutor is required to submit the case to the appropriate court with an accusation.

202. Designation of Court in Decision for Commencement of Trial

The investigating judge determines before which of the authorized courts the case shall be tried.

However, if he deems the Supreme Court to be authorized to handle the case, he sends it to that court through the Public Prosecutor for the execution of the required procedures.

203. Right of Objection to Commencement of Trial

The accused may not oppose a decision pertaining to the commencement of trial.

The Public Prosecutor may demand an urgent exception to a dismissal of the charge by an investigating judge, or to a decision designating a court different from the one set forth in the accusation.

204. Conditions Necessary for Refiling of the Action

After a decision on the dismissal of charges becomes final, the case can be refiled only on the grounds of newly discovered facts and evidence.

205. Accusations by Public Prosecutors in Justice of the Peace Courts

In accusations pertaining to misdemeanors, it is sufficient to indicate the identity of the accused, the article of law violated, and important evidence.

The accused is not served with a copy of the accusation in cases brought in Justice of the Peace Courts.

CHAPTER 5

PREPARATION FOR TRIAL

206. Date of Trial

The date of trial is determined by the Chief Justice.

The following cases are given priority as to date of trial: crimes against the authority of the State and Government; crimes against morals; plundering; highway robbery; kidnapping; and homicide.

207. Summons, Notification and Delivery of Evidence

Summonses are prepared and served, and goods to be used as evidence shall be delivered to the court by the Public Prosecutor.

The presiding judge is authorized to invite some or all of the witnesses and experts for the succeeding trials if it appears that the trial will probably not be concluded within a single day because of the number of witnesses, experts or defendants or because of the length of the hearing.

208. Service of Decision as to Commencement of Trial and Accusation on the Accused

The decision pertaining to the commencement of trial and the accusation by the Public Prosecutor in matters for which no preliminary inquiry is necessary are served on the accused together with a summons directed to him.

209. Appearance of Accused at Trial

In a summons served on an accused who is not arrested, it is stated that he will be arrested or brought by force if he fails to appear without excuse. However, in cases prescribed in Article 225, no such warning is needed. The citation of an arrested defendant is accomplished in accordance with Article 33 by informing him of the date of trial. It is also necessary to ask an accused who has been arrested whether he has anything to say in defense of himself and, if so, what it consists of. This is done by one of the court clerks and a record thereof is kept.

210. Time Between Summons and Trial

The time between service of the summons which shall be served in accordance with the preceding article, and the trial should not be less than one week.

If this period is not observed, the accused may ask for the suspension of the trial at any time prior to the reading of the decision pertaining to the commencement of trial.

211. Invitation of Defense Counsel

The defense counsel, whether designated by the court or by the accused and in the latter case if notice of his appointment has been given to the court, shall be invited together with the accused.

212. Defendant's Claim for Collection of Defense Evidence

The defendant requests the collection of defense evidence and the citation of experts and other witnesses by submitting a pètition to that effect to the court at least five days prior to the date of trial, indicating the facts concerning the mentioned evidence.

The defendant is promptly informed of the decision upon such petition.

When such requests of the defendant are acted upon formally, notice thereof is given to the Public Prosecutor.

213. Direct Invitation by the Accused of a Person Whose Citation has been Refused by the Court

In the event that the court denies an application for the invitation of a witness, the accused may himself invite the person or bring him to the court without submitting any further application.

A person who has been so invited directly by the accused is under an obligation to be present, if his traveling expenses and witness fees are tendered to him at the time of his notification of summons according to a tariff, or deposited in the office of the court.

In the event that the testimony of a person who has been invited directly is valuable in resolving the controversy, the court may, upon request, require the Treasury to reimburse him for any expenses which have been incurred.

214. Direct Invitation by Chief Judge

The chief judge may individually render a decision as to the invitation of witnesses or experts, and as to the collection of other evidence.

215. Notification to the Accused and the Public Prosecutor of Names and Addresses of Experts and Witnesses

Within due time the accused shall notify the Public Prosecutor of the names and addresses of expert witnesses and witnesses who have been invited directly by the accused or will be brought to court by him.

The Public Prosecutor as well shall within due time notify the accused of the names and addresses of experts and witnesses invited by the chief judge or by himself, other than those mentioned in the accusation and at the request of the accused.

216. Hearing of Expert Witnesses and Witnesses Through a Delegated Judge or Interrogatory Commission

If the presence of a witness or an expert at the trial becomes impossible for a long or an indefinite period of time because of illness, defect or any other reason, the court may conduct the hearing of such person through a delegated judge or an interrogatory commission. Where necessary, the testimony is taken after an oath has been administered. This provision also applies to the testimony of experts and witnesses whose presence in the court constitutes hardship because their dwelling places are far distant from the court of trial.

217. Notification of Dates on Which Expert Witnesses and Witnesses will be Heard

Where it will not cause a delay, the Public Prosecutor, the accused and the defense counsel shall be notified of the date on which the experts and witnesses will be heard. Such persons need not be present during the hearing. The record is shown to the Public Prosecutor and the defense counsel.

A defendant under arrest is entitled to be present only at the courthouse of the place of his imprisonment.

218. New Investigation and Inquiry

If a new investigation and inquiry is necessary for the preparation of trial, the provisions of the foregoing articles are applied.

CHAPTER 6

TRIAL

219. Trial Procedure

Trial is held without interruption in the presence of the participants. The presence of the Public Prosecutor and the court clerk are necessary.

The Public Prosecutor does not take part in the trials in Justice of the Peace Courts.

220. Participation of Several Public Prosecutors and Defense Counsels

Where there is more than one Public Prosecutor or defense counsel, they may all participate in the trial together or alternately.

221. Decisions for Suspension and Postponement

Decisions on a demand for suspension of trial are rendered by the court. Decisions for short postponements are rendered by the chief judge. Except in the situation specified in Article 141, engagement of defense counsel does not entitle the accused to claim a suspension of trial.

If the time interval specified in Article 210 has not elapsed, the chief judge notifies the accused of his right to have the trial suspended.

222. Postponement Period

Unless absolutely necessary, a postponement shall not exceed eight days.

223. Non-appearance of the Accused

If the accused does not appear in court, the trial cannot proceed.

If no valid reason for non-appearance is established, either a subpoena or a warrant for his arrest is ordered.

224. Escape at the Time of the Trial

An accused who is present at the court must remain until the end of the trial. The chief judge takes necessary precautions to prevent him from escaping and may also keep him in custody during any postponement.

If the accused escapes or fails to appear at the trial following a postponement, and if he has already been heard, and his further presence is found not necessary by the court, the case may be terminated in his absence.

225. Where Presence of the Accused is Not Necessary

If punishment for a crime consists of light imprisonment, confiscation or a fine, or a combination of these, the trial may proceed without the presence of the accused. In such cases, the accused is informed by the summons of the fact that his non-appearance will not prevent the trial.

226. Where Accused May be Excused From Presence at Trial

Except for crimes carrying heavy punishment, the accused may, upon his own request, be excused from attending the trial.

In such case, if the accused has not been questioned during the preliminary investigation, he will be questioned on the principal facts of the case through an interrogatory commission.

The Public Prosecutor and defense counsel are notified of the questioning date, but they need not be present.

The record comprising the questioning is read during the trial.

227. Authority to Appoint Defense Counsel

The accused is authorized to be represented by defense counsel in cases where the presence of the accused is not necessary.

228. Grounds for Motion for Reinstatement in Cases Tried in the Absence of the Accused

If a trial proceeds in the absence of the accused he may move within a week after notice of the decision to set aside the result of passing the limitation period upon a showing of legal grounds for reinstatement.

However, if the accused is excused from being present in court on his own request, or if he used his right of representation by defense counsel, he may not demand reinstatement.

229. Bringing the Accused to Trial by Force

The court may, at any time, require the presence of the accused, by delivering an order for his appearance and/or a warrant for his arrest.

230. Joinder of Cases

If the court perceives a connection between various cases before it, it may order them to be consolidated for purposes of joint investigation and decision, even though the connection is not one of those mentioned in Article 3.

231. Duty of Chief Judge

The chief judge conducts the trial, questions the accused and hears the evidence.

If an interested party objects to a ruling by the chief judge related to the direction of trial, the court decides thereon.

232. Hearing and Questioning of Experts and Witnesses by Public Prosecutor and Accused

The chief judge, upon the request of both the Public Prosecutor and the accused, may allow them to question experts and witnesses which are named by them. In such case, the Public Prosecutor has the preference to question experts and witnesses designated by himself previously, while the defense counsel has the preference to question experts and witnesses selected by the accused.

If necessary for further enlightenment, such examination may be followed by questions posed by the chief judge to the experts and witnesses.

233. Questioning by Members of Court

Upon request, the chief judge may give permission to the other members of the court to ask questions of the experts and witnesses.

Such permission may also be given to the Public Prosecutor, accused and the defence counsel.

234. Revoking Permission of Hearing and Questioning

The chief judge is authorized to revoke permission to question if one of the parties abuses the right given in sub-article 1 of Article 232.

On instances stated in paragraph 1 of Article 232 and paragraph 2 of Article 233, the chief judge may prevent the asking of unnecessary or irrelevant questions.

235. Questions of Doubtful Permissibility

If there is doubt whether a question is proper or improper, a decision is rendered by the court.

236. Roll-Calling of Experts and Witnesses and Reading of the Decision Concerning the Commencement of Trial

The trial is commenced with a roll-call of experts and witnesses.

This is followed by introduction of the registration of the identity of the accused; reading of the decision concerning the commencement of trial in cases where a preliminary investigation has taken place, or reading of the accusation in cases where there has been no preliminary investigation; and questioning of the accused according to Article 135.

Reading of the decision or accusation, and questioning of the accused are accomplished without the presence of witnesses.

237. Introduction of, and Motions and Decisions Concerning, Evidence

Questioning of the accused is followed by the introduction of evidence.

If a given piece of evidence is challenged, or if the introduction of any evidence necessitates a suspension of the trial, the court renders an appropriate decision.

The court is authorized, upon its own motion or upon request, to order the invitation of witnesses or experts and presentation of other evidence.

238. Scope of Evidence

Evidence includes hearing of all the witnesses and experts who have been invited and the adducing of other proof.

Evidence may not be introduced for the purpose of prolonging the case.

The same principle is applicable where witnesses and experts appear for the first time at the trial, or if their citation is requested, or if other proof is adduced for the first time.

The court can disregard certain evidence with the concurrence of the Public Prosecutor and the accused.

In cases of misdemeanors or a personal action, the court determines the limits of the introduction of evidence, independent of the petition, waiver, and previous decisions.

239. Delay in the Introduction of Evidence

Delay in the introduction of evidence or in the suggestion of a fact to be proved does not justify rejection thereof.

However, the opposing party may ask suspension of the trial for the purpose of obtaining further information if there has been a delay in notifying him of the names of witnesses and experts, or if he lacks information to contest a proposition to be proved because of delay in notifying him of such proposition.

The Public Prosecutor and the accused have similar rights with respect to witnesses and experts invited by the chief judge or the court.

Such requests for suspension are decided by the court at its discretion.

240. Removal of Accused from Courtroom During Questioning

If it appears that there is danger that an accomplice or a witness may not tell the truth in the presence of the accused, the judge may order the accused to be removed from the courtroom during the questioning and hearing.

The substance of the proceedings taken during the accused's absence will be explained to him when he is permitted to return.

241. Release of Witnesses and Experts Who Have Been Heard

After the witnesses and experts are heard, they may leave the courtroom only upon the order and permission of the chief judge.

Before they are released the opinions of the Public Prosecutor and the accused should be asked.

242. Evidence to be Read at the Trial

Instruments and other documents to be used as evidence should be read aloud at the trial.

The same principle is applied to records of previous sentences, summaries of legal records, personal records, and to the records of investigations and inspections.

243. Evidence Consisting of the Testimony of a Single Witness

The witness must be heard during the trial if the evidence of a fact to be proved consists solely in his testimony, based upon personal knowledge.

Previously registered records of the testimony of a witness, or written statements, cannot be substituted for verbal testimony.

244. Where the Reading of Records is Permitted

The reading of records is permitted and is sufficient in cases where the witness, expert or accomplice whose testimony is relied upon has died or has become mentally ill, or cannot be found. The same principle is applied to an accomplice who has been previously convicted.

If the hearing at which the testimony is given takes place after commencement of trial in cases specified in Article 216, or at the time of the preliminary investigations in cases specified in Article 186, the reading of the records thereof is sufficient.

The reading of records as aforesaid, however, is permitted only upon a decision of the court. This decision shall state the reasons for the reading of records, and whether or not the person whose statement is read testified previously. Such ruling has no effect upon the necessity of an oath if the witness or expert is heard again.

245. Statement of Witness Who Declines to Testify

The written statement of a witness who has been heard before trial and who claims his right to refrain from testifying for the first time at the trial, will not be read.

246. Situations Where Previous Testimony May be Read

Where a witness or expert declares that a fact is not remembered by him, the forgotten part of his testimony relating thereto will be read for the purpose of refreshing his memory.

If a contradiction develops between present and previous testimony which cannot be solved without interrupting the trial, previously recorded testimony may be read.

247. Where Previous Statements of the Accused May be Read

Statements of the accused in the record prepared by the judge may be read as evidence of his confession.

If there is contradiction between the present and previous statements of the accused which cannot be solved without the interruption of the trial, the previously recorded statements may be read.

248. Recording of Statements Read

The reading of statements specified in Articles 246 and 247 and the causes therefor will be recorded upon the request of the Public Prosecutor or the accused.

249. Reading of Reports and Other Documents

Experts' reports, doctors' reports of physical examinations, and documents prepared by official departments containing opinions of facts, with the exception of those pertaining to the conduct of the accused, may be read.

If questions are posed pertaining to such reports, written or verbal opinions of the persons who have signed them will be obtained. However, if such reports have been prepared by a committee, the court may suggest that the committee give authority to one of its members to express the view of the entire committee during trial.

250. Opportunity of Defendant to Reply to Witnesses and Documents

After the accused has heard the witnesses, experts, or his accomplice, and after the reading of the documents, he will be asked whether he wishes to reply to such evidence.

251. Statement of Public Prosecutor, Accused and Others

After the introduction and adjudication of the evidence, statements may then be made by the complaining witnesses, then by the Public Prosecutor, then by other interested parties, and after them by the accused.

The Public Prosecutor may reply to the accused, and the accused and the counsel for the accused may reply to the Public Prosecutor. The complaining witnesses and interested parties may reply only with permission of the court. The accused has the right to make the last reply. Even if the accused has been defended by counsel, he will be asked to make a last reply personally if he so desires.

252. Use of an Interpreter

If the accused does not understand Turkish, an interpreter will inform him of the final accusations and defense of the Public Prosecutor and the defense counsel.

If the accused is deaf or dumb and cannot read, he will be treated according to Article 58.

253. End of Trial and Judgment

The trial is concluded with the issuance of a judgment which either acquits or convicts the accused, discontinues the action, or suspends the trial.

If the offense is a kind which necessitates a complaint and the complainant withdraws his complaint, or if for the public prosecution a permission or decision is necessary, or if the accused is mentally sick, the court may discontinue the action or suspend the trial.

254. Weighing the Evidence

The court weighs the evidence submitted in accordance with its assessment of the investigation and the trial.

255. Authority of Criminal Court Concerning Matters relating to Civil Cases

If the criminal nature of an act depends on a civil case, the judge follows the applicable rules of criminal procedure and evidence and not civil law.

The court may, however, suspend the case or give interested parties an opportunity to institute civil actions.

The court may also await the judgment of the civil court concerning these issues.

During the trial the court will decide the ages of the accused and the injured parties according to the census law. Decisions of the court concerning such ages may be appealed, together with the decision on the main issue, to a higher court.

256. Number of Votes Necessary for Decision and Judgment

Decisions and judgments are rendered in unanimity or by the majority of the court. Reasons for the dissenting votes must be entered on the record.

257. Discretion of the Court

The judgment of the court rests on the original charge stated in the accusation.

The court is not restricted by the claims and defenses of the accused or the Public Prosecutor.

258. Changing of the Nature of the Crime Alleged

Unless the accused is previously notified of a change in the legal nature of the offense he was alleged to have committed and is given an opportunity to make his defense, he cannot be convicted in accordance with any article of Law but only with those indicated in the decision for the commencement of trial or in the Public Prosecutor's charge.

This provision is applicable also to cases where new facts, which in accordance with the law constitute matters of aggravation, are adduced during the performance of the trial.

Where the accused, declaring that he could not properly prepare his defense, contests the newly adduced facts which are of a nature to cause his punishment in accordance with a more severe article than was indicated in the decision for commencement of trial or in the Public Prosecutor's charge, or of the nature prescribed in the second paragraph of this article, the court postpones the trial to a later date upon the request of the accused.

Furthermore, as a result of a change in the situation, the court may suspend the case, either upon request or upon its own motion, for the preparation of the accusation and defense.

259. A New Offense of the Accused Found Out During Trial

If during the course of the trial it is found out that the accused has committed an offense different from that with which he is charged, upon the request of the Public Prosecutor and concurrence of the accused, this new offense may be tried with the old one for a joint decision.

This provision shall not apply if the new offense is an Aggravated Felony or beyond the jurisdiction of the court.

260. Points to be Included in the Justification of the Judgment

If the accused is convicted, the justification of the judgment must include the facts which constitute the legal proof of the offense.

If, during the trial, the presence of facts which, by law, require the setting aside or the mitigation or aggravation of the punishment, have been adduced, the justification of the judgment indicates whether or not such assertions were sustained by the court.

Furthermore, justification of the judgment must include the specific articles of the penal law relied upon by the court and the grounds influencing the judge in the determination of the amount of the punishment.

In case the Penal Code has generally limited the application of a less severe punishment to the presence of mitigating circumstances, the court's opinion shall also indicate whether such circumstances were accepted or rejected.

Where parties vested with the right to appeal declare that they waive their right to appeal, indication of the facts constituting the legal proof of the offense and the article applied will suffice.

In the decision of acquittal, the justification includes whether the reason of acquittal is the uncertainty of the commitment of the alleged offense by the accused or absence of a punishment in the law for the said offense.

261. Method of Pronouncing the Judgment

At the end of the trial, or within one week thereafter, the judgment is pronounced by a reading thereof, and by a declaration of the justification of the judgment. Such a declaration is made either by reading the justification or by explaining the main parts.

Reading of the judgment precedes the declaration of the justification thereof. The persons stand while the judgment is pronounced.

If there is a delay in the pronouncement of the judgment, the justification thereof is issued first. If the accused is present during the pronouncement of the judgment, notice of his right to appeal, if any, is orally given to him.

262. Where a Decision for Lack of Jurisdiction Can Not be Given

The court cannot decide that it lacks jurisdiction over a case that has started, by asserting that the case falls within the jurisdiction of a lower court because of the aspects and the nature of the case understood during the trials.

263. Decision of Lack of Jurisdiction of Court

Upon the determination that the offense the accused is alleged to have committed is beyond the jurisdiction of the court, a decision to that effect will be issued and the case transferred to the court of appropriate jurisdiction.

This decision is in the nature of a decision for the commencement of the trial.

Objection thereto may only be taken pursuant to Article 203.

If such a decision is given by a Justice of the Peace and a preliminary investigation had not been undertaken or completed, the accused may demand the gathering of certain evidence before trial within the time period determined by the decision. The chief judge of the court to which the case has been transferred issues a decision concerning this demand.

264. Record of Trial

A record of the trial proceedings is kept, and signed by the presiding judge and recording clerk.

If the presiding judge for any reason cannot sign, then the senior member of the court signs the judgment.

265. Contents of the Record of Trial

The record of trial should include:

(1) Date and place of trial.
(2) Names of judges, Public Prosecutor, recording clerk and interpreters, if any.
(3) Nature and name of the offense as stated in the charge.
(4) Names of accused, their counsel, and the name of the complaining witness.
(5) Whether the trial was open or secret.

266. Other Points to be Included in the Record

The record will clearly indicate the method of conduct and result of the trial, and the main procedures complied with.

It should contain the whereabouts of the documents, summary of all claims, the decision and the holding.

In a trial by the Justice of the Peace, the record will contain the inquiry and summary of the witnesses' statements.

If it is necessary to record a fact that happened during the trial or to include a summary of the testimony, the chief judge orders it. It should also be stated that the record has been read and ratified, and all objections which have been made should be included in the record.

267. Conclusive Force of Record

The validity of any aspect of the trial can be proven only by the record unless that part of the record relied upon is proven to have been false.

268. The Justification and the Contents of Judgment

If the justification for the judgment is not fully included in the record, it shall be so included within three days after the issuance of the judgment.

Judgments and decisions are signed by the judges who participated therein.

If one of the judges is for any reason unable to sign the judgment, the reason therefor is written below the judgment by the chief judge or the senior judge who has participated in the judgment.

The judgment contains the date of the trial and the names of the Public Prosecutor, recording clerk and judges who participated in the trial.

Copies and summaries of the judgment are signed by the chief judge and recording clerk and the official court seal is affixed thereto.

CHAPTER 7

TRIAL OF ABSENTEES

269. Definition

An accused who resides in a foreign country, or whose place of residence is unknown, is an absentee when it is evident that he cannot be brought before the court, or that service of a summons would be useless.

270. Opening of Trial

Trial can be instituted against an absentee for an offense involving fine or confiscation, or both. In this event Articles 271 to 277 are applicable.

271. Period and Method of Service of Summons

If the residence of the accused is unknown, or if it is impossible to extradite him from a foreign country, and the service of a summons on him would be useless under these circumstances, then service of summons is effectuated through attaching a copy thereof to the courthouse wall for a minimum of two weeks.

272. Information Contained in Summons

The summons will include the name, age, occupation, if it is known, the residence and address of accused, day and time of trial and the offense with which he is charged.

Moreover, the summons will state that the accused must stand trial unless he is excused.

273. Defense Representation of Accused

A counsel may appear in court to defend the accused and a statutory relative may so represent him without a proxy.

274. Notice of Judgment

The judgment is notified pursuant to the second part of Article 37.

275. Appeal in Name of Accused

Persons named in Article 273 may file any appeal which the accused himself could have filed.

276. Attachment of Certain Property

Property of the accused in an amount sufficient to cover fines and trial expenses may be attached. Provisions of the Code of Execution and Bankruptcy are applicable to such attachment.

The attachment is set aside as soon as the reasons therefor no longer exist.

277. General Attachment

If attachment is not possible under the preceding article, or if the attachable property does not suffice, then all of the property of the accused in Turkey is subject to attachment. Notice of such general attachment is published in the Official Gazette and, if the court approves, in other newspapers.

After such publication in the Official Gazette, transfers by the accused of his attached property are void against the State Treasury.

The general attachment is set aside as soon as the reasons therefor no longer exist, or as soon as the rights of the State Treasury are protected by attachment of certain goods under Article 276.

Newspapers which published the original order of general attachment will publish notice of the setting aside of the attachment.

278. Action Taken Against Absentee Accused Where no Trial is Initiated

Trial against an absentee accused may proceed only in cases specified in Article 270. In all other instances actions will be taken only to preserve evidence in case the accused later appears.

Such actions will be taken in accordance with Articles 279 and 287.

279. Representation of the Absentee During Preliminary Investigation and Selection of Defense Counsel

Absence of the accused does not bar his being represented during the preliminary investigation.

Statutory relatives of the accused have the right to select such a representative.

Witnesses and experts are examined under oath.

280. Notice of Investigation Matters

An absentee accused is not entitled to notice of the investigation, but the judge may send such notice to his residence, if it is known.

281. Warning to the Absentee

The absentee is warned through newspapers to appear in court or to give his address to the court.

282. Collection of Evidence Regarding the Absentee

After the commencement of the trial, when it becomes apparent that the accused is an absentee, the necessary evidence should be collected by the judges authorized to take depositions.

283. Attachment Where Warrant of Arrest is Required

When suspicious conduct of an absentee accused against whom a public prosecution has been instituted requires the issuance of a warrant for arrest, all of his property in Turkey may be attached by a decision of the judge and presiding judge of the court of first instance.

In the case of an absentee accused who is charged with a crime involving the death penalty or penal servitude as outlined in the first section of the second book of the Penal Code, his property shall be subject to attachment as stated in the preceding paragraph.

284. Publication of Attachment Decision

The attachment decision is published in the Official Gazette and, if the judge or presiding judge of the court of first instance so orders, in other newspapers.

285. Disposition of Attached Property

After preliminary publication in the Official Gazette, the accused cannot dispose of attached property except by dispositions which will be effective upon death.

Notice of the attachment is given to the office in charge of the property of the absentee. This office will take necessary action for the administration of the property of the absentee.

286. Release of Attachment and Publication

When the reasons for attachment no longer exist, the attachment is released.

Publication of the release is made in the same papers where the notice of attachment was published.

287. Action Against Absentee

All necessary measures required in the preliminary investigation are taken upon the filing of a public prosecution against an absentee, in addition to those matters mentioned in the preceding sections.

The decision issued thereafter pursuant to Article 191 may include an annulment or release of the attachment order.

288. Security Bond

The court may grant the accused permission to post a security bond based on specified conditions which will protect the accused from arrest for offenses for which the security has been given. If the accused is convicted and given a punishment which restricts his liberty, or if he prepares to escape, or disobeys the conditions of the security bond, it will be revoked and annulled.

Book III

APPEALS

CHAPTER 1

GENERAL PROVISIONS

289. Right to Appeal

The right to appeal against judicial decisions is open either to the Public Prosecutor or the accused.

The Public Prosecutor may also appeal on behalf of the accused.

290. Right of Defense Counsel to Appeal

The defense counsel may appeal, provided it is not contrary to the explicit desire of the accused.

291. Right of the Legal Representative and Husband to Appeal

The legal representative of the accused or, if a woman, her husband, may appeal within certain prescribed periods. The same appeal procedure applies whether the appeal is made by the accused or by those qualified to make it on his behalf.

292. Procedure Pertaining to Appeals Made by a Detained Person

The detained person may also appeal by making a declaration to the clerk of the court in the area where he is detained. The court clerk prepares a petition in this respect and submits it to the judge or the presiding judge for approval.

In order to comply with time limitations, petitions should be prepared within the prescribed periods.

293. Error in Making an Appeal

An error made in the course of making an appeal shall not prejudice the rights of the applicant.

294. Result of Public Prosecutor's Appeal

The decision against which an appeal is made by the Public Prosecutor may be reversed or changed in favor of the accused.

295. Waiving the Right to Appeal and the Effect Thereof

The rejection of the right to appeal or the withdrawal of an appeal once made is conclusive, even though the period set forth for such appeals has not expired. However, an appeal made by the Public Prosecutor on behalf of the accused cannot be withdrawn without the concurrence of the accused.

The withdrawal of an appeal once made by the defense counsel is subject to the existence of a special power of attorney.

296. Conditions for Withdrawing an Appeal After Proceedings Have Commenced

If the appeal is to be the subject of a hearing, the withdrawal of the appeal is subject to the concurrence of the opponent.

CHAPTER 2

EXCEPTIONS

297. Decisions Against Which an Exception may be Taken

Except as otherwise prescribed by law, exceptions may be taken against the decisions of the investigating judge, those empowered to take depositions, the judge to whom the letter is addressed, and the decisions of the judges of courts of first instance and Justices of the Peace which are not part of the trial proceedings.

Witnesses, experts and other persons may take exceptions to decisions with which they have been concerned.

298. Decisions Against Which Exceptions may be Taken and Decisions Against Which Exceptions may not be Taken

Exceptions are not taken against court decisions except where they pertain to arrest, attachment and third persons.

299. Authorities Reviewing Exceptions and Procedures Applicable

The authorities which are responsible for reviewing exceptions are shown below:

1. Exceptions taken against the decisions of investigating judges shall be examined by the following:
   A. Where the decisions of the investigating judge are not required to be approved, they are reviewed by the chief judge, or the judge of the court of first instance to which the investigating judge is attached.
   B. Where the decisions of the investigating judge become final by approval, they are reviewed by the chief justice of the Aggravated Felony Court to which the investigating judge is attached.
   C. Where the judge making the approval is the chief justice of the Aggravated Felony Court, the exceptions are reviewed by the nearest court handling high criminal matters.

2. Exceptions made against the decisions of a Justice of the Peace are reviewed by the judge or the chief justice of the

101

court of first instance located in the same area of jurisdiction.

Where the cases ordinarily subject to the jurisdiction of the Justice of the Peace are being handled by judges of the court of first instance in a particular area, the chief justice of the Aggravated Felony Court is authorized to review the exceptions. Where the cases ordinarily subject to the jurisdiction of the Justice of the Peace are being handled by one of the members or assistant members of the court of first instance in a particular area, the chief justice of the same court of first instance is authorized to review the exceptions.

3. Reviewing the exceptions taken against the decisions of a delegated or commissioned judge authorized to take depositions is done by the chief justice of the court of first instance in the particular area and the reviewing of exceptions taken against the decisions of the judge or chief justice of the court of first instance is done by the Aggravated Felony Court in that particular area; and the reviewing of exceptions taken against the decisions of the chief justice of the Aggravated Felony Court is done by the nearest Aggravated Felony Court.

Exceptions against a decision are made by submitting a petition to the authority giving said decision, or by making a declaration to the clerk and having him prepare a formal petition in that respect. This formal petition is subject to the approval of the judge or chief justice.

Under urgent conditions, exceptions may be submitted to the authority which will ultimately make the review.

The authority against whom an exception is taken may correct the decision if it deems the exception valid. Otherwise it must forward the exception immediately or at most within three days to the appropriate authority charged with the duty to review.

300. Postponement of Execution

The submission of a petition of exceptions does not postpone the execution of a decision against which the exceptions are taken.

However, the authority which is to review the exceptions or the authority against whose decision exceptions are taken may order the postponement of the execution.

301. Notifying the Opponent of the Exception and the Conducting of an Investigation

The authority which is to review exceptions may notify the opponent in order for the opponent to submit a written reply. If this authority deems it necessary, it may order or conduct an investigation.

302. Decision Regarding the Exception

Except as otherwise prescribed by law, decisions on exceptions are given without hearing. However, if necessary, the Public Prosecutor may be heard.

If the exception is found valid, the authority reviewing the exception may also consider the merits.

303. The Decision Being Final

Decisions on exceptions are final.

304. Procedures Regarding Urgent Exceptions

In cases of urgent exceptions the following procedures are applicable.

Exceptions must be taken within one week after the parties in interest have been notified of the decision in accordance with the provisions of Article 33.

Where the authority against whose decision urgent exceptions are taken rejects the plea of urgency, the submission of the exceptions to the appropriate reviewing authority reserves the afore-mentioned time period.

Judges against whose decisions urgent exceptions are taken cannot change their decisions.

CHAPTER 3

APPEAL

305. Judgments Which Can be Appealed and Those Which Cannot be Appealed

Judgments rendered by criminal courts may be appealed. Sentences restricting liberty for fifteen or more years and death sentences are reviewed by the Court of Appeal on its own motion, without being subject to any charges or expenses.

The following judgments cannot be appealed:

1. Light fines up to and including 20 Turkish Lira.
2. Judgments of acquittal from an offense involving light fines not exceeding 50 Turkish Lira.
3. And judgments which are prescribed by this law or by other laws as final.

The judgments thus given cannot be the basis for a second conviction. However, they may be appealed according to the provisions of Article 343.

306. Appealing Decisions Prior to Judgment

Decisions given before the judgment and forming the basis for the judgment may be appealed together with the judgment.

307. Reason for Appeal

An appeal may be made only for the reason that the judgment is contrary to law.

The non-application or erroneous application of a legal rule is a violation of law.

308. Violation of Law

The following circumstances are considered as absolute violations of law:

1. Failure to convene the court in accordance with the provisions of law.
2. Concurrence of a judge, in passing on the judgment, who is legally prohibited from participation in the duty of judgeship.

3. Concurrence of a judge in passing on the judgment although he is challenged due to a substantial doubt and although such a challenge is accepted, or concurrence of a challenged judge in passing on the judgment by way of unlawful rejection of the challenge.

4. When, in violation of law, the court finds itself competent from the point of jurisdiction to hear a trial.

5. Conducting the hearings in the absence of the Public Prosecutor or of persons whose presence is required by law.

6. Violation of the principles of open session in a judgment passed as a result of an oral hearing.

7. A judgment which does not include justification for the result reached.

8. The restriction of the right to defense, by a court decision, on points which are important for the judgment.

309. Violation of Rules Which are in Favor of Accused

Violation of the rules which are in favor of the accused does not give the Public Prosecutor a right to have the judgment reversed against the accused.

310. Conditions for and Period of Appellate Request

The request for appeal must be made within a week after pronouncement of the judgment by either submitting a petition to the court which gave the judgment or by making a declaration to the registration clerk and having him prepare the necessary formal documents which are to be approved by the judge or chief justice.

If the judgment has been pronounced in the absence of the accused, the period for appeal starts from the date of notice to him.

Persons appealing judgments which are not related to misdemeanors must deposit 10 Turkish Lira within a week. The beginning date for said week is the day on which the petition of appeal is submitted or the declaration is made.

According to the result of the appellate review, the deposited sum, if the requested review is valid and justified, will be refunded; if not, it will be recorded as revenue to the Treasury.

Persons submitting a certificate obtained from Municipalities or Village Councils indicating that they are needy, and Public Prosecutors, are exempted from depositing money.

Judgments rendered by Justices of the Peace which can be appealed may be appealed by the Public Prosecutor assigned to the criminal court of first instance or to the Aggravated Felony Court within the jurisdictional department of the Justice of the Peace Court which rendered the judgment within one month after the judgment is pronounced.

311. Running of the Appeal Period Within the Period of Reinstatement

For judgments which are not in favor of the accused and which are pronounced in his absence, the period for a reinstatement request runs during the period for appeal. If the accused makes a request for reinstatement, taking into consideration the probability of his request being refused, he must make a request within the periods set forth for appeal by either filing a petition or by making a declaration to the registration clerk. In this event, procedures pertaining to appeal are postponed until a decision regarding reinstatement is given.

Provisions for depositing money must be performed within a week after the person requesting appeal has knowledge, according to the provisions of Article 33, of the decision refusing the reinstatement or denying the urgent exception requests.

If the course of appeal is chosen without making a request for reinstatement, it indicates that the right for reinstatement is renounced.

312. Effect of an Appellate Petition

The appellate petition filed within the periods set forth prevents the judgment from becoming final.

If the reasons for the judgment have not been given to the party requesting an appeal, he will be so notified within a week after the court has knowledge of the appeal.

313. Appellate Petition and the Points it will Contain

The party making an appeal will indicate in his appellate petition or declaration or appellate brief those portions of the judgment to which he objects and the grounds on which he requests the judgment to be reversed.

In the reasons for appeal it should be indicated whether the objection involves a violation of legal rules regarding procedure or other legal provisions. In the first case, events contrary to law are to be explained.

314. Voluntary Appellate Petition

If the reasons for appeal are not indicated in the appellate petition, an appellate brief containing the reasons will be submitted to the originating court before the expiration of the period set forth for appellate petitions or, if the reasons for the judgment have not yet been indicated, within a week after the notification of such reasons.

Failure of submission of the appellate brief, or the omission of the reasons in the appellate petition or declaration, do not bar appellate review.

If the appeal is made by the accused, the petition is signed by the accused or by his counsel.

If the accused does not have a defense counsel, he may declare his reasons for appeal to the registration clerk, who will prepare the necessary record. This record must be approved by the chief justice or judge.

315. Refusal of an Appellate Request by the Court Which Issued the Judgment

If the appellate request is made after the expiration of the legal period, or the money which is one of the conditions for appeal is not deposited, the court whose judgment has been objected to shall, by decision, reject the appellate petition.

The appealing party, within a week after notice to him of the decision of refusal, may apply to the Court of Appeal for a decision to be given in this respect. In that event the file is submitted to the Court of Appeal. However, execution of the judgment cannot be delayed for such a reason.

316. Notification and Answer Pertaining to Appellate Petition and Appellate Brief

The copy of the appellate petition and the copy of the appellate brief, if there is one, regarding the appellate request which the originating court has not rejected under the provisions of Article 315, will be issued to the opposing party of the one requesting the appeal. The opposing party may submit his written answer within a week.

If the opposing party is the accused, he may also submit his answer by making a declaration to the court clerk who accordingly prepares the record. After the bill of answer is submitted or the period for answer has expired, files pertaining to the case are forwarded by the Public Prosecutor to the Chief Public Prosecutor's Office in order to be submitted to the Court of Appeal.

317. Rejection of the Appellate Request by the Court of Appeal

If the Court of Appeal determines that the provisions pertaining to the submission of the appellate petition or pertaining to the depositing of the money have not been observed, the appellate request is rejected. Otherwise, the Court of Appeal reviews the case.

318. Hearing During Review of the Judgment Pertaining to Major Offenses

The Court of Appeal conducts its review regarding judgment pertaining to major offenses by conducting a hearing either upon the request made in the appellate petition of the accused, or on its own motion. The accused or, upon his request, his counsel, is notified as to the date of the hearing. Either the accused himself or his counsel who has a power of attorney may be present at the hearings.

If the accused is under arrest, he cannot make a request for being present at the court.

319. Procedures Pertaining to Hearings

Hearings at the Court of Appeal begin with an explanation of the case made by the member reporter. This member should prepare his report, which is signed and placed in the files, before the hearing.

Following the explanation made by the member reporter, the Chief Public Prosecutor, the accused and his counsel take the stand and present their assertions. Among these parties, the party who made a request for appeal is heard first. The accused has the last word.

320. Points that will be Reviewed by Court of Appeal

The Court of Appeal is entitled to review on points indicated in the appellate petition and in the appellate brief and, if the appellate request is based on omissions regarding court procedures, on the facts declared in the appellate petition and on other violations of law, even if they are not mentioned in the appeal, which will have a bearing on the judgment.

It is not necessary to indicate new grounds other than those mentioned in paragraph 2 of Article 313 in order to confirm the assertion regarding the appeal.

However, if such grounds are introduced they are accepted.

321. Reversal of the Judgment by the Court of Appeal

The Court of Appeal reverses the judgment to which objection is raised on the points where the law is violated.

If the violation of the law that caused the reversal of the judgment was based on the facts determined as the basis of the judgment, related proceedings are also reversed at the same time.

322. Circumstances in Which Appellate Court will Decide on the Merits of the Case and Correction of Decision

If a judgment was reversed because of a violation of law applied to the facts which were determined as the basis for the judgment, the Court of Appeal in the following situations gives a complete decision on the merits of the case in place of the originating court:

1. If a decision for an acquittal or for the cessation of the investigation is necessary without further clarification of the fact.
2. If the Court of Appeal concurs with the assertion of the Chief Public Prosecutor for the application of the minimum degree of punishment prescribed by law.
3. If the law has been erroneously applied.
4. If the provisions of law regarding court fees and expenses are violated.

In cases other than the above, the Court of Appeal forwards the file to the originating court or to another nearby court of parallel jurisdiction for review of its own decision and for a new judgment.

If the offense involving a punishment is within the jurisdiction of a lower court, the Court of Appeal may transfer the matter to that court.

The Chief Public Prosecutor may protest the decision given by one of the Criminal Departments of the Court of Appeal at the General Criminal Board of Court of Appeal within thirty days after the court decree has been submitted.

The correction procedure against the decision of Criminal Departments or General Criminal Board is possible only in case of omissions, during appellate review, of points specified in an appellate petition, in an appellate brief or in a notification, and of errors which will directly affect the essence of the judgment.

The right to request a correction decision lies with the Chief Public Prosecutor. Upon this request, appellate review is conducted by the department or board which has rendered the decree under consideration. Local Public Prosecutors, on their own motion or upon the request of the parties concerned, draw the attention of the Chief Public Prosecutor to the case and forward the files. If the Public Prosecutor does not consider the request of the parties concerned as requiring a correction of the decision, he cannot delay the execution of the decree. The Chief Public Prosecutor reviews the matter and if he does not consider the request for correction valid, he orders the execution; otherwise, he orders the suspension of the execution to the Public Prosecutor concerned. He then takes the required measures. If the request for the correction of decision is rejected, a second request for correction cannot be made.

323. To Which Authority Decisions Which have been Reversed for Reasons of Non-Jurisdiction will be Forwarded

If the judgment has been reversed due to the court's unlawful decision regarding its jurisdiction over the case, the Court of Appeal will submit the case to the court which has primary jurisdiction.

324. Pronouncement of Judgment

Judgment is pronounced in accordance with the provisions of Article 261.

325. Effects of a Reversed Judgment to Other Accused Persons

If the judgment has been reversed in favor of the accused because of the violation of law regarding the application of the punishment, and if the reversed points are applicable to accused persons who have not made a request for appeal, they benefit from the reversal of the judgment just as though they had made a request for appeal.

326. Rights and Responsibilities of the Court Which will Rehear the Case

The courts have the right to insist on their first judgment when their judgment is reversed by the Court of Appeal, but they are obliged thereafter to abide by decisions given by the General Criminal Board of the Court of Appeal.

If the judgment is appealed only by the accused or by the Public Prosecutor on behalf of the accused or by the persons mentioned in Article 291, the newly passed sentence cannot exceed the sentence set forth in the first judgment.

Book IV

BOOK IV

NEW TRIAL AND WRITTEN ORDER

327. Reasons for a New Trial in Favor of Accused

A case which has been concluded with a final judgment will be tried anew in favor of the accused under the following circumstances:

1. If any document used in the hearings and which had an effect on the outcome of the judgment is fraudulent.

2. If it is discovered that any witness or expert who has been heard under oath has testified or used his vote deliberately or negligently against the accused contrary to the facts in a way affecting the judgment.

3. Excepting errors caused by the accused personally, if any of the judges participating in the judgment, while performing his duty, has committed an error calling for a criminal prosecution and a conviction.

4. If the judgment of the criminal court is based upon the judgment given by a civil court and this judgment was reversed by another judgment which became final.

5. If new facts or new evidence are presented which, when taken into consideration solely or together with the evidence previously stated, are of a nature to require the acquittal of the accused or the application of a provision of law involving a lighter punishment. However, as to judgments pertaining to misdemeanors, only facts and evidence which were not previously known to the accused or which were not previously adduced by the accused without any fault on his behalf may be declared.

328. Postponement of Execution of Judgment

Request for a new trial does not postpone the execution of the judgment. However, the court may grant a postponement or stay of execution of the judgment in its discretion.

329. Circumstances Which do Not Bar a New Trial

The execution of the judgment and even the death of the accused do not bar a request for a new trial.

In the event of the death of the convict the wife or husband, ascendants or descendants, sons or daughters, and brothers or sisters of the deceased may request a new trial.

330. Reasons for a New Trial Unfavorable for the Accused

A case which has been concluded by final judgment may, under the following circumstances, be reheard by way of a new trial against the accused or the convict:

1. If a document, which during the hearing was used in favor of the accused or the convict and which had an effect on the outcome of the judgment, is fraudulent.

2. If it is discovered that any witness or expert who had been heard under oath had testified or used his vote, deliberately or negligently, in favor of the accused or the convict, contrary to the facts in a way to affect the judgment.

3. If any of the judges participating in the judgment has committed, while performing his duty, error requiring a criminal prosecution and punishment.

4. If the accused has made a reliable confession after he has been acquitted.

331. Circumstances Which do not Permit a New Trial

A new trial is not permissible for the changing of the punishment if the change is to be made within the limits of the same article of law.

332. Conditions for Accepting a Request for New Trial Due to an Offense Involving a Punishment

Request for a new trial due to the presence of an offense involving a punishment can only be accepted when there is a final judgment regarding the offense or when it is not possible to conduct or continue prosecution and investigation for reasons other than lack of evidence.

333. Provisions Applicable to the Request for a New Trial

General provisions which are applicable to the procedures for appeals are also applicable to the procedures regarding a new trial.

334. Contents of the Request for a New Trial and the Procedures Thereof

The request for a new trial must contain the legal grounds and evidence regarding the request.

The accused or the persons indicated in paragraph two of Article 329 may request a new trial by submitting a petition to the court or by making a declaration to the clerk of court and having him prepare the necessary formal documents in this respect.

335. Decision Involving the Invalidity of the Request for a New Trial and the Related Authority

The court against whose judgment an objection is raised by a request for a new trial, decides whether this request is valid or not. When a request is made for a new trial, regarding a judgment reviewed by the Court of Appeal as a result of an appellate petition, if the grounds for requesting a new trial are other than those specified in Article 327 (3) or Article 330 (3), the right to render a decision regarding a new trial belongs to the court whose judgment was appealed.

The decision as to the validity of the request for a new trial is given without a hearing.

336. Invalidity of a New Trial Request and Procedure Applicable in Case Request for a New Trial is Accepted

If the request for a new trial is not made in accordance with the procedures set forth by the law or if no legal reason has been indicated to justify a new trial or any evidence to confirm it, the request is rejected as not being valid.

Otherwise, notice of the request for a new trial is given to the opposing party within a set time limit, in order to determine his opinion.

337. Collection of Evidence

If the court accepts basically the request for a new trial, it assigns, if necessary, an interrogatory commission for the collection of evidence.

The court decides whether or not the witnesses or experts to be heard will be administered on oath.

During the collection of evidence, provisions applicable to the preliminary investigation regarding the presence of the parties in interest are applied.

After the collection of evidence is completed, the Public Prosecutor and the accused are invited to state their opinions and considerations within a time limit set forth.

338. Rejection of Request for a New Trial on the Basis of No Grounds: the Hearing

If the reasons presented for a new trial are not found sufficient or if the circumstances indicated in Article 327 (1, 2) and 330 (1, 2) are understood to have no bearing on the judgment previously given, the request for a new trial is rejected due to lack of a legal basis without having a hearing.

Otherwise, the court grants a new trial and a new hearing.

339. Review Without Hearing of the Request for a New Trial

If the convicted person is dead, the court without having a hearing, but if necessary, after the collection of evidence, decides either for an acquittal of the convicted person or for the rejection of the request for a new trial.

In other cases also, the court, if there is sufficient evidence, rules on the acquittal of the convicted person without having a hearing.

However, if the proceedings had been commenced by a Public Prosecution, a decision may only be given with the concurrence of the Public Prosecutor.

With the decision for acquittal, the court also annuls the previous judgment.

A person requesting a new trial may demand the publication of the previously annulled judgment in the Official Gazette, as well as in other papers, if the court deems it necessary. Publication expenses are paid by the Treasury.

340. Urgent Exceptions Taken against Decisions Regarding a New Trial

Urgent exceptions may be taken against decisions regarding the validity of a request for a new trial.

341. Judgment to be Given at the End of a New Hearing

At the conclusion of a new hearing the court either approves or annuls the previous judgment, and in the latter case, gives a new judgment.

The new judgment given upon a request for a new trial made only by the convicted person or on his behalf by the Public Prosecutor or by the persons mentioned in Article 291, cannot contain a punishment heavier than the punishment prescribed by the previous judgment.

342. Fines to be Paid for Unjustified Requests for New Trial

If the convicted person requesting a new trial proves to be unjustified and his request is malicious, he is sentenced to a heavy fine of 25 to 200 Turkish Lira.

343. Reversal by a Written Order

If the Minister of Justice is informed as to the violation of law in the decisions or judgments given by judges or courts which become final without review by the Court of Appeal, he may give a written order to the office of the Chief Public Prosecutor to apply to the Court of Appeal for the reversal of the decision or judgment. In this written order legal grounds for the reversal are indicated.

The Chief Public Prosecutor quotes only the legal grounds in his notification and submits the file to the Court of Appeal.

The Court of Appeal, if it finds the stated legal grounds valid, reverses the decision or the judgment.

Judgments given by courts which relate to the merits of the case reversed in the above manner, do not prejudice the rights of the parties in interest.

If the reversal is in their favor, the following procedures are applicable:

1. If the grounds for reversal involve the entire removal of the punishment of the convicted person, the Court of Appeal indicates in its decision that the sentence previously passed will not be served.
2. If the grounds for reversal do not involve the entire punishment but merely the removal of a certain portion of the

punishment of the convicted person, the Court of Appeal specifies in its decision the punishment to be applied.

3. If the reversal pertains to the decisions of the examining magistrate or the court decisions not related to the merits, then the decision will be given according to a new review and investigation.

BOOK V

PARTICIPATION OF PERSONS WHO HAVE
BEEN INJURED BY THE OFFENSE

CHAPTER 1

PERSONAL ACTION

344. Relief for an Offense by Personal Action

In the following cases the person injured by the offense may sue the offender directly by bringing a personal action without demanding the Public Prosecutor's participation:

1. " The offense of threat " indicated in the last paragraph of Article 191 of the Turkish Criminal Code.
2. " The offense of breaking into a house," indicated in Article 193, paragraph 1 of the Turkish Criminal Code.
3. " The offense of disclosing secrets of third persons," indicated in Articles 195 and 197 of the Turkish Criminal Code.
4. Physical violence indicated in the last paragraph of Article 456 and in paragraph 1 of Article 459 of the Turkish Criminal Code.
5. " The offense of libel and slander " indicated in Articles 480 and 482 of the Turkish Criminal Code.
   (However, if these offenses are of the nature indicated in Articles 164 and 166 of the Turkish Criminal Code, they are prosecuted by the Public Prosecutor.)
6. " The offense of causing loss and damage to third persons " indicated in Article 516, paragraph 1 and in Article 518 of the Turkish Criminal Code.
7. " The offense of unfair competition " indicated in Articles 64 and 65 of the Turkish Commercial Code.
8. Offenses related to copyrights, patent rights and property rights related to fine arts, etc., indicated in special regulations and laws.

If the victim has a legal representative, the right of bringing a personal action belongs to such representative.

If the victim is a society or a business association and is qualified to bring an action in legal matters, the right of bringing an action is by the persons representing such society or business association.

123

345. Right of Personal Action by More Than One Person With Respect to the Same Offense

If two or more persons have the right to bring a personal action for the same offense, they can invoke their respective rights severally.

However, if the personal action was brought by one person, the other persons in interest may enter the case, but they can only participate in the case at whatever phase it stands when they enter.

All decisions taken, even those related to the merits, will affect the accused in his favor against the parties who have not brought personal actions or who are in the same status.

346. Right of Action of Public Prosecutors from Point of Public Interest

Public Prosecutors may file a public prosecution upon the request of the parties in interest and under the circumstances indicated in Article 344 only if there is public interest in the case.

347. Status of the Public Prosecutor in Trials Related to Personal Actions

Public Prosecutors are not obliged to participate in trials regarding personal actions.

Public Prosecutors may start a public prosecution by making a declaration at any phase of the case until the judgment becomes final.

When the Public Prosecutor takes one of the appeal courses, it indicates that he has instituted a public prosecution. When the Public Prosecutor commences a public prosecution, the proceedings from that time are conducted according to the provisions regarding the intervention of the victim in the second chapter of this code.

348. Plaintiff Bringing Defense Counsel with Him or Sending a Counsel to Represent Himself

The plaintiff may be present at the trials personally and may have a lawyer or defense counsel with him or may be represented by a lawyer or defense counsel who has a power of attorney. In the latter case, any notice to his lawyer or his defense counsel is considered as having been made to the plaintiff.

349. Depositing a Bond by the Plaintiff

In cases where, upon the demand of the defendant, the plaintiff is required to deposit a bond to cover expenses according to the provisions of the Code of Civil Procedure, he shall deposit a bond to cover the expenses of the Treasury and the accused.

This bond may be in cash or Government bonds or securities.

In determining the amount of bond and the time limitations for depositing bonds and in considering legal assistance, provisions pertaining to civil matters are applied.

350. Filing of Personal Action

Personal actions may be filed either by making a declaration to the court clerk, for which a formal petition will be prepared, or by submitting a petition, either to the investigating judge or to the Justice of the Peace depending upon the nature of the offense. The declaration or the petition must be in accordance with the provisions of Article 193, paragraph 1. Two copies of the petition are attached to the original copy.

In the declaration or petition, the nature of the claimed right must be indicated.

351. Notice to Accused, Public Prosecutor and to Party Secondarily Liable

If the personal action is filed in accordance with the aforesaid article, notice of the declaration or the petition is given to the accused and to the party secondarily liable—if there exists such a party against whom an action is taken—in order that they may state their answer in the prescribed time limit. Notice is also given to the Public Prosecutor so that he can be informed of the action.

352. Decisions of the Investigating Judge and the Justice of Peace

After the accused or, if there is any, the party secondarily liable has forwarded his answer or after the expiration of the prescribed time limit, the investigating judge or the Justice of the Peace either opens the hearings or rejects the action.

353. Procedures After Commencement of Proceedings

The procedures from that point are conducted in accordance with the provisions regarding a public prosecution.

A matter that is being prosecuted in the form of a personal action cannot be combined with an offense which is being heard by a court which has jurisdiction over high criminal matters.

354. Rights of Person Taking Personal Action

The plaintiff in a personal action is summoned and heard in the same manner as a Public Prosecutor in a public prosecution. All matters of notice to the Public Prosecutor required in a public prosecution must also be given to the plaintiff bringing a personal action.

However, notice of a summons is made by the court clerk.

There must be at least a period of a week between the date of the notice of the summons to the plaintiff, and the date of the hearing.

The plaintiff, his counsel or his lawyer may obtain information from the files with the permission of the judge and in the presence of the court clerk.

355. Determination, Summoning and Invitation of Required Witnesses and Expert Witnesses

The chief justice determines in advance the persons who are to be called to trials as witnesses and expert witnesses.

The plaintiff, as well as the accused and the party who is secondarily liable, if there is any, has the right in the same degree to summons or invite witnesses directly.

356. Right of the Accused to Have a Defense Counsel with Him or to Represent Himself

The accused may be present alone or may have a lawyer or a defense counsel with him, or he may be represented by a lawyer or a defense counsel with a power of attorney.

The court may give orders to the plaintiff as well as to the accused and may serve a subpoena on the accused for his personal presence at the trials.

357. Cross Action of the Accused

The accused may bring a cross action against the plaintiff and may request his conviction as long as he is not informed that the trial is over.

In this case the original and the counter actions are adjudged jointly.

Waiving the original action does not bar trial and judgment regarding the counter action.

358. Decisions Regarding Personal Actions to be Given Together with Judgment

If the accused is convicted, the court may also render a decision regarding the personal claim.

However, if the investigations pertaining to the presence of the loss or the amount thereof will extend the trial or delay the judgment, the court may include only the punishment in its judgment and may indicate in the judgment that the plaintiff may apply to the civil court for his claim.

359. Cessation of Procedure

If the court, after investigation and study of the case, determines that the facts established relate to offenses not involving the court action indicated in this chapter, it renders a decision for the cessation of actions pertaining to the case and submits the files to the Public Prosecutor.

360. Right of the Plaintiff to Appeal

In matters which are instituted by bringing a personal action, the plaintiff may take the appeal courses which are granted to the Public Prosecutor during a public prosecution.

The same provisions are applicable to requests for a new trial indicated in Article 330.

The provisions of Article 294 are also applicable to requests made by plaintiffs.

Request for an appellate review or for a new trial is made by submission of a petition by the plaintiff or by his lawyer or by making a declaration for which a formal petition will be prepared. This formal petition is submitted to the chief judge or the judge for approval.

The documents mentioned in Article 316 are submitted to the Public Prosecutor, pursuant to procedures exercised in public prosecutions, and forwarded by the Public Prosecutor.

The court clerk gives notice of the appellate petition and the appellate brief, if there is any, to the party opposing the one requesting appellate review.

361. Waiving His Case

The plaintiff may waive his case at any time up to the time the judgment is pronounced. However, the provisions of Articles 460 and 489 of the Turkish Criminal Code are reserved.

The plaintiff is considered to have waived his case when he does not personally appear in the hearings of cases in which the Public Prosecutor has not intervened and participated or does not have himself represented; or when he does not come to any one of the sessions, though the court had ordered him to be present in person; or when he does not comply with the time limitation prescribed by the court although the court had informed him that he would be considered to have waived his personal claim in case he does not comply within the prescribed time limitation.

The plaintiff may request restitution within a week after notice of the judgment adjudged in his absence, pursuant to the conditions in Articles 41 and 42.

362. Waived Cases Cannot be Refiled

A waived case cannot be refiled.

363. Inheritors' Right to Pursue

If the plaintiff dies, his heirs may continue the prosecution.

The provisions regarding libel and slander of the Turkish Criminal Code are reserved.

364. Waiver of the Case

Notice of waiver of the case is given to the accused and to the person secondarily liable.

CHAPTER 2

INTERVENTION IN A CASE

365. Intervention in Public Prosecution

Any person who is injured by the offense may, at any phase of the investigation, intervene in the public prosecution.

Those so intervening in a public prosecution may also adjudicate their personal claims.

366. Procedure of Intervention

Intervention is made by submission of a petition to the respective authority or by a declaration made to the court clerk from which the court clerk then prepares an official petition. This petition is approved by the chief judge or the judge.

The proper authority, having heard the Public Prosecutor, decides whether the request for intervention is acceptable.

The intervenor is not required to deposit a bond.

367. The Intervenor's Rights

From the moment the request for intervention is accepted, the intervenor enjoys the same rights as those of a prosecutor of personal claims.

368. Effect of Intervention on Proceedings

Intervention does not interrupt the proceedings.

The hearing, the date of which is determined, and the other procedures of the trial, are executed on the prescribed day, even if the intervening person cannot be summoned or informed due to lack of time.

369. Intervenor's Exceptions Against Decisions Given Before Intervention

Decisions given before intervention, notice of which are given to the Public Prosecutor, are valid even in the absence of notice to the intervenor.

129

When the time limit for the Public Prosecutor to appeal against this decision expires, the intervenor also loses the right to appeal.

370. Notice of Judgment to Intervenor

If the intervenor or his representative does not attend the trial, notice of the judgment will be given to the intervenor.

371. Intervenor's Application for Appeal

The intervening person may appeal independently of the Public Prosecutor.

If the decision appealed from is reversed upon the application of the intervenor, the Public Prosecutor should prosecute again.

372. Invalidation of Intervention

If the intervenor withdraws his claim, his intervention is invalidated.

Book VI

ADMINISTRATION OF TRIAL AND PROCEDURE OF DELIBERATION

CHAPTER 1

PUBLICITY AND DISCIPLINE OF TRIALS

373. Publicity of Trials and Conditions for Closed Session

Trials are open to the public. However, the court may decide to have partly or completely closed sessions for reasons of public morals and security.

The decision for a closed session and its legal grounds are explained openly; the judgment should also be pronounced openly.

374. Secrecy of the Session Held to Decide on Closed Sessions

Pursuant to the foregoing article, the request for a closed session is held in secret, upon request, or on the court's own motion.

375. Mandatory Closed Session

Trials of children who are not over fifteen years of age must be conducted in closed sessions.

The judgment also is pronounced in closed session.

376. Appending the Decision for a Closed Session and Reasons Therefor into the Trial Record

The decision for a closed session and the reasons therefor are appended to the record of the trial.

377. Permission for Entrance into Closed Sessions

The court may permit certain persons to enter closed sessions. In this case the chief judge warns them not to disclose the matters which necessitated the holding of a closed session.

Publication of trials conducted in closed sessions is forbidden.

If an openly conducted trial is deemed to be harmful to the dignity and pride of the accused or of the plaintiff, or to be contradictory to morals or to be provocative of public excitement, the court rules for the prohibition of the trial's publication in the press and openly pronounces its decision.

Those publishing open or closed trials contrary to the

prohibition, will be sentenced to a light imprisonment up to one week and to a light fine up to 50 Lira.   This decision is final.

The provisions of this article are also applied to the procedure of civil trials.

378. Discipline of the Trial

Discipline of the trial is maintained by the chief judge.

The chief judge removes from the courtroom any person violating the discipline of the trial.

The chief judge does not permit in the courtroom minors whose presence is deemed inappropriate.

379. Disciplinary Punishments

Persons who direct an impertinent word or action toward the court are immediately sent to a detention house upon the decision of the court.   They are questioned within twenty-four hours, and sentenced by the court to a light imprisonment up to one week, or to a light fine up to 25 Lira, as disciplinary punishment.   This decision is final.

380. Procedure Regarding Offenses Committed During the Trial

In case a person commits an offense during the trial, the court determines the incident, prepares a record thereof and sends it to the appropriate authority; the court may arrest the person as well, if it deems it necessary.

CHAPTER 2

PROCEDURE OF DELIBERATION AND VOTING

381. Judges Authorized to Participate in Trials and Judgments

Legally prescribed numbers of judges must participate in sessions and judgments.

For trials which will not terminate in one session, alternate members may be assigned, to replace members who will probably be absent, and to participate in voting.

382. Judges to Participate in the Deliberation

Only the judges who will participate in the judgment may be present at the deliberation. The chief judge may permit law graduates who are under court training to be present at the deliberation.

383. Administration of the Deliberation

Administration of the deliberation and the arrangement of matters to be discussed are controlled by the chief judge.

384. Obligation to Participate in Voting

No judge may abstain from participation in the voting on the ground that he is in the minority on some matter.

385. Obtaining the Majority When the Votes are Divided

When the votes are divided, the vote most unfavorable for the accused is added to the next unfavorable vote until a majority vote is obtained.

The chief judge collects the votes, beginning with the junior member, and he himself votes last.

Book VII

SPECIAL PROCEDURES OF TRIAL

CHAPTER 1

PENAL DECREES BY JUSTICE OF PEACE

386. Penal Decrees to be Passed without Hearing

The Justice of the Peace, by issuing a decree without a hearing, may rule on misdemeanors which rest within the jurisdiction of Justice of the Peace Courts.

Only the punishment of a light fine or light imprisonment up to three months and suspension of a certain profession or trade, when necessary, may be adjudicated by this penal decree.

387. Disadvantage of the Omission of Hearing

If the Justice of the Peace considers it disadvantageous to impose punishment without a previous hearing, he assigns a date for a hearing.

388. Matters Required to be Written in Decree

The penal decree includes, in addition to the punishment given, the committed offense, the applied articles of law, the evidence, and the fact that an exception can be taken within eight days starting from notice of the decree, by submitting a petition to the Justice of the Peace Court, or by informing the court clerk, who will prepare a formal petition thereof; otherwise the penal decree will be executed. This formal petition is submitted for the judge's approval.

The convicted person may waive his exception before expiration of the period.

389. Finality of Decrees to Which no Proper Objection is Made

Penal decrees which are not objected to in the prescribed period become final.

390. Objection to Decree

Upon objection to the decree, a hearing is held. However, if the accused waives his objection prior to the hearing, no hearing is held.

The accused may be represented by his defense counsel at the hearing. The judge is not bound by the previous decision when ruling on the exception.

391. Rejection of Exception

If the accused fails to appear at the hearing without an excuse and does not send a defense counsel, his exception is rejected without any review.

If the accused's request for reinstatement, due to the expiration of the period for exception against the penal decree, is accepted and if his exception is rejected due to his failure to appear, he can no longer request reinstatement.

Chapter 2

PROCEDURE OF CONFISCATION

392. To Whom Confiscation Request is Made

If a decision regarding the confiscation, destruction or withdrawal from use of certain goods authorized in accordance with the provisions of Article 36 and of other Articles of the Criminal Code and of other special laws was not given together with the principal decision, the request to be made by the Public Prosecutor or the plaintiff regarding the establishment of the above precautions apart from all other proceedings will be directed to the court having jurisdiction over the main case.

Confiscation of property, possession or use of which is in and of itself not an offense, but which for some other reason is nevertheless subject to confiscation, is decided by the Justice of the Peace without any hearing. Interested persons may apply for urgent exceptions to this decision.

393. Provisions Regarding the Hearing and Decision of Confiscation

Provisions regarding trials are applied to the hearing and decision of confiscation.

If possible, those who have a right to the goods which are to be confiscated, destroyed or taken out of use are also summoned to the hearing. They have the rights of an accused and may be represented by an attorney having a power of attorney.

Failure to comply with the summons neither postpones the proceedings nor voids the judgment.

394. Those Vested with the Right of Applying for Appeals Against the Decision of Confiscation

The Public Prosecutor, the plaintiff and the persons named in Article 393 may apply for appeals against decisions of confiscation.

Book VIII

EXECUTION OF PUNISHMENT AND
COURT EXPENSES

Chapter 1

EXECUTION OF PUNISHMENT

395. Conditions for Execution

Sentences cannot be executed until they become final.

396. Basis of Execution and the Person to Carry Out the Execution

The execution of the punishment is carried out by the Public Prosecutor on the basis of the judgment which is issued by the court, and approved by the chief judge or the judge, that it is a true copy and that it is subject to execution.

397. *Repealed.*
[7–9–1953.]

398. *Repealed.*
[7–9–1953.]

399. Reasons for Postponement of Execution of Punishment Restricting Liberty

Execution of punishments restricting the liberty of those who are suffering from mental disease is postponed until the patient has recovered.

The same provision is applied in the event of any other illness which will constitute a great danger to the life of the convict in the event of execution of a judgment restricting liberty.

Execution of a punishment restricting the liberty of pregnant women and for women who have just given birth is postponed for six months after the date of birth of the child. If the child dies or is given to another person other than her mother, the punishment is executed two months after giving birth.

400. Postponement of Execution upon the Application of the Convict

If the execution of a punishment restricting liberty for two years or less, not being a term of heavy imprisonment, will cause serious

145

damage, not compatible with the purpose of the punishment, to the convict or to his family, the execution of the punishment may be postponed upon request of the convict. The period of postponement shall not exceed four months.

The acceptance of the request for postponement may depend upon the posting of a bond or fulfilment of another condition.

401. Process to be Applied to Convicts who Fail to Appear for Imposition of Punishment or who are Suspected of Flight

If the convict does not comply with the summons issued for the execution of his punishment, or if he is suspected of flight, the Public Prosecutor may issue a subpoena or a warrant of arrest to provide for the execution of the punishment.

If the convict has fled or hidden, the Public Prosecutor may, for the same purpose, issue a warrant of seizure.

402. Uncertainty of Interpretation of the Judgment and on Execution of the Punishment

In case of uncertainty of the interpretation of the judgment or on the calculation of the punishment; or in case it is asserted that the punishment should not be partly or completely executed, a decision thereon is requested from the court.

The same provision is applicable to objections against the rejection of the request for the postponement of the execution of punishment in accordance with Article 399.

These applications do not postpone the execution of the punishment. However, the court may direct the postponement or the suspension of the execution.

403. Addition of Punishments Included in More than One Sentence

If there are various final sentences regarding one person and if it is seen that the principle of the addition of punishments has not been applied, a request is made to the court for a decision to determine a punishment in accordance with the related provisions of the Penal Code.

404. Deduction of the Hospitalization Period from the Punishment

If, due to illness after the execution of the punishment has started, the convict is transferred from the prison hospital to another hospital, the hospitalization period is deducted from the punishment.

However, if the convict himself has purposely caused the illness in order to obtain the suspension of execution, he cannot benefit from this provision.

In this latter case the Public Prosecutor is responsible to obtain the appropriate decision of the court.

405. Authority to Render Decisions at the Time of Execution and the Procedure Thereof

The decisions which are to be obtained from the court at the time of execution of the punishment (Articles 402–404) are rendered without hearing. Before the decision is rendered, the Public Prosecutor and the convict are given time to submit their assertions.

In case a punishment is required to be determined pursuant to the principle of addition of punishments in accordance with Article 403, the court which decided the heaviest punishment, or if the punishments are of the same nature the court which decided the greatest amount of punishment, but in this event if more than one court have jurisdiction over the case the court which passed the latest dated sentence is authorized to decide in this respect. If one of the sentences is passed directly by the Court of Appeal, this court is authorized to apply the principle of addition of punishments.

Urgent exceptions can be taken against the above decisions given by courts other than the Court of Appeal.

CHAPTER 2

COURT EXPENSES

406. Determination of Court Expenses

Judgments, decrees and decisions regarding the discontinuance of investigation also determine the party who will pay court expenses.

The judge or the chief judge determines the amount of expenses and the amount of money that one party should pay to the other. The execution of the judgments regarding the collection of personal rights is subject to the provisions of the Law of Execution and Bankruptcy.

Decisions regarding court expenses due to the Government are executed in accordance with the provisions of Article 97 of the Law of Judicial Duty Tariff, No. 2503.

407. Liabilities of the Convict

All expenses, including the preparation expenses of the public prosecution, are paid by the convict. If the convict dies before the sentence becomes final, his heirs are not liable for the payment of expenses.

408. Expenses in Cases of Partial Conviction for More Than One Offense and of Conviction of More Than One Person for the Same Offense

If the person against whom legal proceedings were taken for more than one offense is sentenced for part of the offense, he is not liable to pay the expenses of the hearings on the offenses for which he is acquitted.

Persons sentenced as being accomplices to the same offense are liable for the court expenses as joint sureties for each other's debts.

This provision is not applicable to expenses of the execution of the punishment and arrest.

409. Expenses in Cases of Acquittal or Dismissal of Charges

The person who obtains a decision of acquittal or a dismissal of charges pays only the expenses caused by his own negligence.

148

The Government Treasury may be made liable for the expenses which a person was previously obliged to pay.

410. Expenses in Counter Actions of Libel

Suspending punishment of one or both parties in a prosecution of libel or slander does not preclude liability of one or both parties to pay the expenses.

411. Expenses in Cases of Malicious Prosecution and Aspersion of Felony

A person who, by malicious prosecution or aspersion of felony, or by culpable negligence, makes a false report and instigates legal investigation, may be charged with the payment of expenses incurred by the Government Treasury or by the accused, after judicial hearing.

If the court has not yet heard the case, the decision in this respect is given by the investigating judge authorized to order the opening of the final investigation upon the assertion of the Public Prosecutor.

In case the charges are dismissed at the end of the preparatory investigation, the decision in this respect is given by the Justice of the Peace upon the request of the Public Prosecutor.

Urgent exception can be taken against such decisions.

412. Expenses in Case of Renouncing Personal Prosecution

If a decision on discontinuing of the investigation is given because the person who made a request regarding his personal rights withdraws his request, expenses are paid by the plaintiff.

413. Expenses in Case of Conviction Upon Personal Prosecution

In personal prosecutions the convict pays the necessary expenses of the plaintiff.

If the accused is partly convicted, the court determines the shares to be paid by the plaintiff and the accused as court expenses and expenses made by both parties.

If a decision of dismissal of charges, or acquittal of the accused or dropping of the investigation is given, expenses which the accused incurred become payable by the plaintiff.

If there is more than one plaintiff and more than one accused, they are liable for the payment of the expenses as joint sureties for one another.

Expenses mentioned in this article also include expenses for necessary travel and compensation to be paid to witnesses and experts in order to substantiate personal rights. The same provisions are applicable to the fees to be paid to defense counsel.

414. Expenses Resulting from Filing Personal Action and Public Prosecution

If a public prosecution is filed under Article 168 and if it results in the dismissal of the charges against the accused or acquittal of the accused or discontinuance of the investigation, the provisions of paragraphs 2–5 of Article 413 are applied to the applicant.

However, the court or the judge, if the circumstances require, may adjudge that the applicant will be partly or completely free from liability for the payment of expenses. The court or the judge hears the applicant before ruling on expenses, except where the applicant has no right of intervention.

415. Expenses Resulting from Appeals

The appellant will pay all expenses resulting from his withdrawal or from the rejection of his petition. If the Public Prosecutor has made the appeal, the Government Treasury is liable for the expenses which the accused has to pay.

In case the applicant's request for appeal is partly accepted, the court divides the expenses as deemed appropriate.

The same provisions are applicable to expenses resulting from the request for a new trial regarding a trial which is concluded by final judgment.

The expenses resulting from the request for reinstatement, provided they are not caused by baseless opposition of the other party, are to be paid by the applicant.

BOOK IX

RESTITUTION OF RIGHTS LOST THROUGH CONVICTION

RESTITUTION OF RIGHTS LOST THROUGH CONVICTION

416. Authority

Petition for the restitution of abridged rights is submitted to the court handling aggravated felonies located in the area where the sentenced person is domiciled.

417. Documents to be Attached to the Petition

The following documents are attached to the petition:

1. A copy of the judgment indicating the conviction;
2. Documents certifying that the petitioner's punishment has been executed or dropped on legal grounds, their dates, certifying that the court expenses and, if adjudged, personal rights, have been paid;
3. Documents showing his good conduct to imply his repentance for the offense for which he was sentenced.

418. Review and Decision

Upon this petition, the court assigns one of its members as reporter. The reporter obtains the criminal records of the sentenced person, collects necessary information and, having computed whether or not the time limitations prescribed in Articles 122 and 123 of the Criminal Code have expired, submits the files to the Public Prosecutor's office.

The court decides without a hearing, upon the Public Prosecutor's opinion substantiated by evidence. This decision can be appealed to the Court of Appeal.

419. Rejection and Renewal of Requests

In case the petition is rejected, a new request for the restitution of rights lost through conviction cannot be made, unless the time limitations prescribed in Articles 122 and 123 of the Criminal Code are observed once more, starting from the date the decision of rejection became final.

Restitution can always be requested in case the rejection is based on the lack of, or improper form of, some documents.

420. Publication of Decision of Restitution

The final decision regarding the restitution of rights lost through conviction is published in the Official Gazette, if the petitioner so desires.

THE LAST ARTICLES

THE LAST ARTICLES

421. Aggravated Felonies According to This Law

Aggravated felonies according to this law are felonies punishable by death, heavy imprisonment and imprisonment for more than five years.

422. Repeal of Laws

Excepting offenses punishable by heavy punishment, for which the provisions of this code are applicable, legal proceedings and investigation in accordance with the provisions of this code concerning provincial governors, governors of counties and governors of townships, for their personal felonies not arising from their official duties or not committed during the performance of their official duties, are taken by the Public Prosecutor and the investigating judge of the county to which the governor of a township is attached and of the province to which the governor of a county is attached and the capital of the province nearest to the province where the governor's office is located. The initiation of the trial regarding the offenses subject to the provisions of this article is the responsibility of the appropriate court of the locality where the prosecution is being conducted.

423. Vacation

Authorities and courts handling criminal matters are closed for vacation from July 20 to September 5 each year.

The Ministry of Justice specifies the conduct of hearings on the preparatory and preliminary investigation involving arrested persons and of other urgent matters during the vacation periods.

During the vacation period, the Supreme Court reviews only those matters which are subject to the law regarding court procedures pertaining to the flagrant offenses and to offenses involving arrested persons.

Time limitations do not run during a vacation. These time limitations are observed as extended for three days after the vacation is terminated.

424. Terms and Expressions

The terms and expressions used in this Code are substituted for the old equivalent terms and expressions which are used in the Turkish Criminal Code.

425. Effective Date of This Code

This code becomes effective four months after its publication date.

426. Authority to Execute This Code

The Council of Ministers is responsible for the application of the provisions of this code.